QUEEN VICTORIA
AT OSBORNE

QUEEN VICTORIA AND PRINCE ALBERT AT OSBORNE IN OCTOBER 1859

Queen Victoria at Osborne

Arnold Florance

Foreword by the late
EARL MOUNTBATTEN OF BURMA
KG, PC, GCB, OM, GCSI, GCIE, GCVO, DSO, FRS

English Heritage
London

NOTE

Readers of this book who wish to have further details of the artefacts mentioned in it would do well to purchase *Osborne House: Principal Items on View*, and the souvenir guidebook, *Osborne House*, both published by English Heritage.

First published by Yelf Brothers 1977
Second edition published by English Heritage 1987
Printed in England for HMSO by W.J. Linney Ltd, Mansfield
Dd 8975225 C300 5/87
ISBN 1 85074 154 9

Contents

Illustrations

Foreword

by the late Earl Mountbatten of Burma
Admiral of the Fleet,
Governor and Lord Lieutenant of the Isle of Wight

I am glad to commend this fascinating account of Queen Victoria's visits to the Isle of Wight in the nineteenth century. It is of particular interest to me as Kent House, which she gave to her mother the Duchess of Kent, passed by inheritance through Princess Louise, Duchess of Argyll, to my mother Victoria, Marchioness of Milford Haven (Princess Louis of Battenberg).

My family lived there from the end of 1914 until just before my father died in 1921, and so we all got to know the Osborne Estate very well.

From May 1913 to the end of 1914 I was a Naval Cadet at the Royal Naval College, Osborne, built in the grounds and making use of the large stableblock of Osborne House.

So I grew up knowing Osborne House and its surroundings well and, therefore, specially welcome this book.

Mountbatten of Burma
1977

Introduction

It may well be asked, "Why another book on Queen Victoria?" To answer this question I must point out that the object of this book is to describe her life at Osborne from the time that it was designed and built under the supervision of the beloved Prince Consort until her death surrounded by her children, grandchildren and great-grandchildren. Unlike Balmoral, Buckingham Palace and Windsor Castle, which since her death have been altered to suit later generations, Osborne ceased to be a royal residence. It remains therefore a perfectly preserved example of the Queen's life and character.

Visitors to Osborne may wonder what went on there during the Queen's long reign. Victoria herself might well have taken for a motto that of her great predecessor, Elizabeth I—*semper eadem* (always the same). Whether facing poets or cabinet ministers, bishops or faithful servants, her character and behaviour remained unchanged, and what went on at Osborne went on also in her other homes. Balmoral and Osborne shared on account of their inaccessibility the same strong objection from her ministers, who more than once referred to Osborne as the great enemy; and although in her later years the journey was comparatively quickly accomplished, fog in the winter and gales in the summer sometimes prevented easy travel. And there was no telephone service at Osborne until 1900.

As time went on, the Queen's regular visits, accompanied by an entourage of perhaps a hundred people, became an established feature of the Isle of Wight, and her presence loomed large in local life. Many still living have memories or traditions of her progresses in the Island, and of her interest in the lives of her tenants. Because of her fondness for Osborne, Victoria was perhaps more closely associated with the Isle of Wight than with any other part of her Dominions. It is here, therefore, that we can best study her way of life; and since the opening to the public of the private suite on the first floor of Osborne House, by her great-granddaughter, Queen Elizabeth II, we can appreciate even more clearly the private character and achievements of the great lady who gave her name to the Victorian Age.

Arnold Florance
1977

1 Early Days at Norris Castle

My sad childhood

Among the visitors to the Isle of Wight, early in the last century, might be seen a widow lady, dressed in dark colours and wearing a large hat trimmed with black ostrich plumes. She was accompanied by her little daughter, a child of about eleven years of age, usually dressed in a simple cambric frock and pelisse ornamented with a frill of fine needlework. As was the fashion then, her hair was parted in the middle, and a few artificial curls hung on either side of her face.

Sometimes on their outings they were accompanied by a shrewd-looking lady of middle age, thin and angular, and smelling strongly of caraway seeds. Between these two ladies German was spoken, but the child spoke English in a clear precise voice "without the trace of an accent." This small party, with its few attendants, consisted of the Duchess of Kent; her daughter, the Princess Victoria, heir presumptive to the throne; and her governess, Baroness Lehzen.

These early visits of Princess Victoria, as a little girl, to the Isle of Wight were made when there was a vast growth in the number of travellers to the increasingly popular seaside resorts around the country. Victoria's grandfather, George III, had helped to increase their popularity over half a century before, when he went bathing with his family at Weymouth, and ate his breakfast informally out of doors, a custom to be continued by his granddaughter throughout her long reign. Later, Victoria's father, the Duke of Kent, sought out a residence at Sidmouth where he believed the sea air would benefit his wife and child, though he himself died shortly afterwards of pneumonia.

Apart from health considerations, seaside resorts were proving more attractive than their inland counterparts, for the simple reason that there was much more to do. There were the delights of regattas and reviews, and the pleasant sights of yachts, frigates, and fishing boats; while for those in search of the picturesque there could be added the variety of sea and coast. "The form and grimace of tea-drinking" could be replaced by the more vigorous pursuits of bathing, sailing, and expeditions, some of quite an arduous nature. The spirit of adventure was abroad, even among those of modest means.

The Isle of Wight at the time of Queen Victoria's childhood had much to offer in this way. Its beautiful and varied scenery never failed to entrance the writers of the many topographical books published about this time. "Such is the purity of the air, the fertility of the soil, and the beauty and variety of the landscape," wrote one enthusiastic traveller, "that it has often been styled *The Garden of England*. Parties of pleasure are on that account frequently made to it . . . while

1

it abounds with delightful scenes which recommend it to the attention of the artist." Indeed, there was a sufficient number of wild aspects of scenery to satisfy the most fastidious traveller in search of the picturesque. There were at Niton the Sandrock Springs, which were reputed to contain more mineral than the celebrated chalybeate springs at Tonbridge; among the pilgrims to these were Victoria and her mother.

A journey from London to the island in the early part of the century could take as long as seven hours, but once paddle steamers were in operation the journey was a good deal less tiring and much more comfortable. The roads on the whole were bad and not so numerous as now. Some guidebooks advised travellers to be careful of their horses and the springs of their carriages, and when in doubt to dismount and walk. I do not suppose that the Princess did very much walking, but I suspect she did enough to allay the myth that she had been born with weak legs.

Whatever may have been the cause, the young Princess enjoyed her holidays in the island and was able to forget the dullness of what she called her "rather sad childhood." She retained memories which must have contributed to her choosing as a married woman to make her holiday home in the island. That her mother had decided on visiting the Isle of Wight had been brought about in rather interesting circumstances. The Duchess had on her staff a comptroller, Sir John Conroy, a rascal and intriguer who felt, in his vulgar fashion, that the Duchess had more than an ordinary liking for him. She certainly listened very closely to his advice. Whatever may have been his motives, it was he who persuaded the Duchess to holiday in the Isle of Wight, where for many years he occupied Osborne Lodge, an old thatched cottage which afterwards came into the possession of the Queen, and which stood on the present site of Osborne Cottage.

The nearest residence to his home which was suitable for the Queen was Norris Castle. This was a mock Gothic edifice built by Lord Henry Seymour about 1800, commanding a fine view of the Solent from pleasantly laid-out grounds. Here Victoria could ramble about as she pleased, and ride out without an equerry. There are records of the little blue-eyed girl wandering on the shore, chatting to sailors and fishermen. One romantic American records that he saw her with eyes filled with tears, seated in Arreton churchyard, while her mother read the popular and very pious story of "The Dairyman's Daughter."

One of the first public duties of the future Queen was in 1831, when she laid the foundation stone of East Cowes Church. A lengthy and elaborate ode in the classical manner to celebrate the occasion was published by Yelfs of Newport, the established local family of printers.

In August of that year the Duchess and the Princess again visited the island, landing at Ryde Pier from the Commissioner's yacht. Lord Vernon fired a salute and manned the yards of his yacht. The Duchess and the Princess were travelling to Norris Castle, where they stayed for approximately two months. The castle had recently become vacant on the death of Lord Henry Seymour. Upon their arrival at Norris Castle salutes were fired by revenue cutters lying in Cowes roads, and by the battery at the Yacht Club. The Princess made a tour of the western part of the Island, including Yarmouth. Ryde, Ventnor, and Newport were also visited. This stay was interrupted by a visit to London, at the beginning of September, to watch King William IV's Coronation Procession on 8 September.

Meanwhile changes were taking place which altered the whole course of Victoria's life. The Princess had a nervous liking for her rough-mannered uncles, and they had a warm spot for her, although they were loath to recognise her close connection with the throne. Their mutual dislike of the Duchess of Kent maintained an unpleasant atmosphere of hostility. George IV died in 1830, and the new King, William IV, was sensitive to the fact that his brother's death brought his niece nearer in the line of succession to the throne.

Conroy had unwisely advised the Duchess to request William to create her Regent to Princess Victoria, as next in line of succession. The King naturally refused to allow this, and to demonstrate his hostility the Princess was assigned a place in the Coronation Procession behind her uncles. There is a story that, as a result of this insult, the Duchess confined her weeping daughter to a lobby at the top of the stairs at Norris Castle.

The journey to London itself had not been without its rebuffs. Conroy unwisely took it upon himself to order ships in Portsmouth Harbour to fire a salute as the Duchess' party disembarked. William was greatly annoyed and ordered the "popping to stop forthwith." A year or two later "to pop or not to pop" became a constant bone of contention.

It was two years before the Princess again visited the island. On 1 July 1833 she and her mother, attended by Sir John and Lady Conroy, arrived at Portsmouth at 4pm. The Admiral, Sir Thomas Williams, took the party in his barge to the royal yacht *Emerald* (see Chapter 10), which was then towed by a steamer to Cowes, arriving at about 7pm. The party then proceeded by carriage to Norris Castle.

A week later the Duchess with the Princess returned to *Emerald*, which was towed to Southampton by the *Medina* steam-packet. The following day they paid a short visit to Ryde. Excursions were also made to the "back" of the island. On Sunday they attended divine service in the old church at Whippingham (see page 79), and were present at the consecration of the new church at East Cowes. On 18 July they again went on board *Emerald* and were towed by the *Messenger* steamboat to Portsmouth to visit Nelson's *Victory*.

On 29 July *Emerald* was taken in tow by *Messenger* to Weymouth at the start of a tour of the West Country. On 8 August Princess Victoria and her mother returned to Norris Castle, again aboard *Emerald*; they stayed there until 6 November.

By 1833 the Princess had been encouraged to keep her own diary, a task which she religiously observed for practically the whole of her life. In this diary Victoria refers to her visit in that year:

> Dear Emerald . . . We set off [from Portsmouth] and arrived at Cowes at about 7. We were most civilly received. Cowes Castle, the yacht-club, yachts, etc., etc., saluting us . . . We drove up in a fly to Norris Castle, where we lodged two years ago, and where we are again living. My cousins and my brother [her stepbrother Charles, Prince of Leiningen] were *delighted* with it.

By an interesting coincidence they had tea in old Osborne House, and attended church at Whippingham. Did Victoria ever imagine that one day she would become owner of Osborne Estate, and that in the church there would be a family pew? It was after this visit that an incident occurred which is often misrepresented as having nearly ended Victoria's life: "Dear *Emerald*" collided with a hulk outside Plymouth, breaking her mast in two places. No one was hurt, although melodramatic stories got about of the falling of rigging close to the Princess and of her being snatched clear by the pilot, Mr Saunders.

Visits to the island ceased for some time after 1833.

At five o'clock in the morning of 20 June 1837, Princess Victoria began her long reign as Queen, and later Empress. One thing is certain, she never forgot her holidays in the island, where she could escape for even a short time from the restrictions of the Court. The desire to make a home there was partly brought about by the recollections of her happy days at Norris Castle.

2 A Home of Our Own

Albert and I talked of buying a place of our own which would be so nice

William IV was on the throne for only seven years, at the end of which time Queen Victoria began her long reign of sixty-four years. For the first ten years after her accession events crowded in upon the young Queen, and she threw herself wholeheartedly into the new life she had to follow. But in spite of the fatherly assistance of Lord Melbourne she found it hard to learn the life of Court and State, with its intrigue and gossip. She enjoyed the balls and parties and the royal progresses, but she often felt a sense of loneliness and isolation, and seemed quite willing to consider a partner with whom she could share her private, as well as her public, life. She finally chose as her husband Prince Albert of Saxe-Coburg-Gotha. There is no doubt that from the first it was a love match, and that at the time that Osborne House was planned they shared the same tastes and ideals.

When she came to the throne the Queen had few royal residences where she and her husband could make their home, and these were limited in convenience and comfort. Hampton Court had ceased to be occupied after the reign of George II; Kensington Palace, where the Queen was born and largely brought up, could scarcely be called a "palace." Of course there was Windsor Castle, which had so long been the favourite home of Victoria's grandfather, George III, but this building required a thorough cleaning. There were smells, the source of which remained untraced for a long time. "There will be terrible stinks there one day" warned Sir Jeffry Wyatville, the architect who transformed the castle in 1824. There was Buckingham House, purchased by George III, but although an official residence of the royal family, the Queen described it in 1845, when she already had four children, as "not *decent* for the occupation of the Royal Family." The nurseries were in the attics and, on more than one occasion, members of the public got in and slept in the private apartments. What was even worse, the drainage was bad, and there was evidence of an open sewer. No wonder the Queen took an interest in lavatories throughout her life, and the Consort devoted his energies later on at Osborne to the disposal of sewage.

George IV had bequeathed to Victoria that elegant "seraglio," Brighton Pavilion, but this building, because of its position, completely denied the Queen any privacy; and the public did not hesitate when the opportunity occurred to thrust their faces under the royal bonnet. Thus there was little of comfort for the young Queen, with her rapidly growing family.

Meanwhile the Prince soon found that his role as Consort and husband was a

5

difficult one, particularly in public. He hated the noise of London and Court society, and although a good dancer he was quickly bored at balls and receptions, preferring music to gossip and chess to chatter. He was a countryman by nature, brought up as he had been in the Rosenau, where he had spent a free and happy childhood.

During their travels about the country the Queen had not failed to notice the privacy and tranquil life enjoyed by her aristocratic subjects on their fine estates. To own a home of her own was what she most desired, and she expressed this wish to her husband during a cruise on the south coast. This took place in August 1843, when the royal couple were on their way to visit the King and Queen of France at the Château d'Eu, near Dieppe. At Southampton they boarded the new royal yacht *Victoria and Albert* and crossed to Cowes on 28 August. The same day the yacht took them to Ryde, where they drove through the town on their way to visit Lord Harcourt at "St Clare." On the 29th they went briefly to Appuldurcombe and on to East Cowes, calling at Norris Castle, before embarking for Dartmouth, en route for France.

No doubt this visit recalled memories of the Queen's childhood visits to Norris, but in spite of old associations any plan to purchase this estate was rejected. "How odd," observed a member of the royal household, "that the Queen and the Prince should not have chosen Norris Castle. Such a splendid place, so regal; besides, the Queen stayed there as a child, and it has many historic associations. Altogether a most suitable place as a royal residence." "No, they would have nothing to do with Norris Castle," replied George Anson, the Prince Consort's private secretary, "they prefer—so they said—any cottage-looking thing to a castle."

However, Victoria and Albert had no need to look far, for nearby was Osborne House and its estate, which promised to be much more the sort of place the royal family wanted. Osborne House was a typical Georgian house of moderate size, but was not as distinguished as some of the more noted Isle of Wight manors. The estate had been owned by the Mann family and their descendants since the time of Charles I. The visitor to the island, whose commendation of it was quoted in the previous chapter, described the house in 1789 as being "one of the best chosen residences in the island. On a fine spacious lawn, that leads to the sea. . . . The views . . . are as extensive as they can be. . . . The building is very large, and has all its offices behind it. The inside is equally convenient and roomy; and is now receiving considerable improvements." In spite of the reference to the size of the building the rooms appear to have been somewhat small. Yet, whatever its demerits, the Queen declared it was just what she wanted—solid and homely and commanding superb views.

The Queen's physician, Sir James Clark, came to satisfy himself that the air would be suitable, and in the autumn of 1844 the Queen rented the property

THE ORIGINAL OSBORNE HOUSE

for £1000 for a year's trial.

One part of the estate, the house and a park of 200 acres, was owned by Lady Isabelle Blachford, a widow of a descendant of the Mann family; for this a price of £30000 was asked. The other part consisted of Barton Manor, Barton Wood, a house named "Dashwoods" and Little Shambles Farm. These were owned by Winchester College, and were offered to the Queen for £20000. They were, however, leased until 1862 to the Rt Hon George Seymour and Sir George Francis Seymour, and to enable the Queen to take possession it was necessary to pass in 1845 a private Act of Parliament (8 & 9 Vict c20), the Preamble to which states that "it would greatly improve the . . . Osborne park Estate, and would render the occupation and enjoyment thereof by Her Majesty much more comfortable and commodious if Her Majesty were to acquire the absolute ownership of . . . Barton Manor and Barton Wood with the sea shore adjacent thereto." Thanks to negotiations undertaken by Sir Robert Peel, the Queen was able to purchase the house and park for £26000, and the Winchester College property for £18000 plus a rent charge of £113-16s-0d a year and 13s-4d a year to the Bishop of Winchester. It is to the credit of the royal couple that the money for the purchase came out of the careful saving and new economies which the Prince had achieved.

On 25 March 1845 the Queen wrote to her uncle, Leopold of the Belgians: "You will, I am sure, be pleased to hear that we have succeeded in purchasing *Osborne* in the Isle of Wight, and if we can manage it we shall probably run down there before we return to Town, for three nights. It sounds so snug and nice to have a place of *one's own*, quiet and retired, and free from all Woods and Forests, and other charming Departments who really are the plague of one's life." In another letter the Queen expressed again that she was "perfectly satisfied with their new home," and in the spring of 1845 she and their children spent their first holiday as a family in the island. "[W]e were so occupied, and so delighted with *our new* and really delightful *home*," she wrote to Lord Melbourne, "that we hardly had time for anything; besides which the weather was so beautiful, that we were out almost all day. The Queen refers Lord Melbourne to Mr Anson for particulars of the new property, which is very extensive, as she is not at all competent to explain about acres, etc. But she thinks it is impossible to imagine a prettier spot—valleys and woods which would be beautiful anywhere; but all this near the sea (the woods grow into the sea) is quite perfection; we have a charming beach quite to ourselves. The sea was so blue and calm that the Prince said it was like Naples. And then we can walk about anywhere by ourselves without being followed and mobbed, which Lord Melbourne will easily understand is delightful. . . ."

One early visitor was the toothless old King of Holland, who, in spite of his handicap, talked a great deal. But the visit went off "wonderfully well in our little house."

At this time the Queen's happiness was marred by the resignation of Sir Robert Peel; she listened with a sad heart to the explanation given by the minister who had played such a large part in the purchase of Osborne. She wrote to Lord Melbourne, explaining that in view of the state of his health she could not ask him to form a new government, and she received a reply, the sentiments of which were echoed by later ministers: the journey was so long, and he had such a horror of the sea, that a voyage from Southampton to Cowes or from Portsmouth to Ryde seemed to him a prospect as formidable as a voyage across the Atlantic.

Charming and informal as the Queen's holiday home appeared to be, filled with her personal belongings and furnished with simple chintz-covered furniture, it was not a spacious house, and there was limited room for the reception of visitors and ministers. It was not surprising, therefore, that shortly after their spring visit the royal family were preparing to say goodbye to their "dear little home." Plans had been made to begin a fine new building, the foundation stone of which was laid on 23 June 1845. The old house was finally pulled down; all that remains of it is the elegant porch which is now incorporated in the wall of the nursery garden.

In July 1845 the Queen wrote that the Princess was "in rapture over the sea-shells" and that "the dear Prince is constantly occupied in directing the many necessary improvements which are to be made, and in watching our new house, which is a constant interest and amusement."

The first section of Osborne to be erected was what is called the Pavilion wing, which contained mainly the private apartments, including a nursery for the children and limited accommodation for the staff. Previously the staff had been housed in cottages on the estate.

The Prince Consort did not merely supervise the design of the new house but was largely responsible for it. He had already compared the Solent on a fine day to the Bay of Naples, so it is not surprising that a building in the Italian style should suggest itself. Moreover, there was at that time a strong fashion for designing houses according to the type of local landscape. In 1841 Richard Brown published a book on this subject, showing by means of engravings how a house in the form of a medieval castle would require a steep bluff; a classical mansion, smooth lawns; one in Elizabethan style, a meandering stream backed by woodland. Perhaps encouraged by these principles, and his own love of Italian art, the Prince designed their new home in a Palladian style, complete with loggias and towers or campaniles. Indeed, there is some resemblance to the Palace of Caserta. The constructor and adviser was the well-known London builder, Thomas Cubitt, "than whom," as Queen Victoria said, "a better, kinder man did not exist." Cubitt had introduced into building construction the use of cast-iron beams, and this technique was used at Osborne so that the structure should be fireproof.

9

The Pavilion was designed to take full advantage of the fine views, particularly of the Solent. At the same time, because the area was small, it was hoped that there would be a certain intimacy which would be lacking in a large house. Very little has since been moved or altered, so that the sort of life which Victoria and Albert lived on the island becomes evident to present-day visitors.

The furnishing of the house proceeded slowly—bits and pieces were added to it until the late sixties. Meanwhile, rather than buy an upright piano the Prince hired one by the quarter from a firm in Newport. I presume that he did this in holiday time for use by the royal children. The sale of the Brighton Pavilion to the Town Commissioners in 1849 enabled the royal couple to spend £29 000 on furnishings at Osborne. (The Queen was appalled to learn from Albert, who examined the accounts with an eagle eye, that the maintenance of the Pavilion since her accession had cost more than £24 000, none of which had been paid by the nation.) Most of the furniture was designed and supplied by Hollands of London, and some of the statuary came from the Great Exhibition of 1851.

The twin Italianate campaniles form a noticeable feature of the house. The first to be erected was the flag tower, and the later one contains the striking clock. This clock was originally built for George III when he lived at Kew. It was converted from a single dial to four dials with an additional mechanism from the Brighton Pavilion. Thus Victoria possessed at Osborne relics of two former royal homes.

The approach to Osborne at this time was along the Royal Walk, an avenue of ilexes, which wound its way towards the house. It did not approach it in the more direct way that the present entrance does.

The grounds around the house were still in a rough state, and the development and landscaping of them were done largely under the Prince's supervision—a task he obviously enjoyed. The ground was sown with grass and became a playground for the royal children. The extent and variety of trees at Osborne owes much to the enthusiasm of the Prince Consort at this time. In 1849 alone he planted evergreen oaks, Scotch firs, cork oaks, and *pinus matadima* (stone pine), in addition to climbing plants against the kitchen buildings, heather upon the terraces, and evergreen shrubs between the stables and clock-tower. The arrival of important personages, birthdays and other special occasions were all excuses for planting trees. If the weather was not suitable for a tree to be actually dug in, a mark was placed in position and the planting postponed to a more seasonable time. Many of the trees have survived in spite of age and decay.

Many famous people planted trees at Osborne, but Garibaldi, so much admired for his work for Italian freedom, was not among them. The Queen regarded him as a revolutionary. It so happened, however, that while Garibaldi was in England he was invited to the island by General Seely, later Lord

OSBORNE HOUSE UNDER CONSTRUCTION

Mottistone, at a time when the Queen was in residence at Osborne. She heard of the visit, sent for General Seely, and demanded to know why he had done this. Garibaldi, she said, had even been asked to plant a tree at Mottistone. To this General Seely replied that what he did on his own estate was his affair, and he did not question what went on at hers. The Queen, in a better humour, smiled in recognition of her mistake and the interview closed quite amicably.

At the north of the new building was a natural declivity and this formed the basis for a terraced garden, again in the Italian manner. In it were subsequently placed one of the undistinguished sculptures from the Great Exhibition, which served the Queen as a perpetual reminder of Albert's greatest achievement.

Before house or garden was complete, however, the royal family moved into their new home. The first night, 15 September 1846, is described to us very vividly by Lady Lyttleton:

> Nobody caught cold or smelt paint, and it was a most amusing event coming here. Everything in the house is quite new, and the dining-room looked very handsome. The windows, lighted by the brilliant lamps in the room must have been seen far out to sea. After dinner we rose to drink the Queen's and Prince's health as a *house-warming*, and after it the Prince said very naturally and simply, but seriously, "We have a hymn" (he called it a psalm) "in Germany for such occasions. It begins"—and then he quoted two lines in German which I could not quote right, meaning a prayer to "bless our going out and coming in." It was dry and quaint, being Luther's, but we all perceived that he was feeling it.
>
> Much the best part was . . . Lucy Kerr (one of the maids of honour) . . . throwing an old shoe after the Queen as she entered for the first night . . . this being a Scotch superstition. She wanted some lead and sundry other charms, but they were not forthcoming.

The additional accommodation for the household was not finished until 1851. Even then it did not completely cater for all requirements; for large functions a marquee had to be erected on the lawn outside the house.

Undoubtedly one of the finest rooms is the Council Chamber, in which are the Sèvres portraits of the Queen and Prince, based on work by Winterhalter, and both still look quite young. Beyond lies the small audience room where the Queen received so many important ministers and famous visitors during her long lifetime.

With the completion of the Household block: ". . . a great dinner in the open air was given to all the workmen, both of the building and property, in which 270 participated. After dinner there was dancing and games until sunset, with the families and workmen joining in, and what is worth mentioning: not the slightest irregularity occurred."

Charles Greville commented rather sourly that "the building was very ugly"

THE COUNCIL CHAMBER (WEST END) IN 1867

and that "a great deal of money has been spent on it," but he added with some satisfaction, "it is not the nation's."

In subsequent years additional wings were completed and the original estate of about 1000 acres was increased by various purchases to over 2000 acres by 1864.

A small volume, dated 1880 and published by Yelf's, reveals the absorbing interest which Prince Albert showed in the development and improvement of Osborne House and the estate. The title page reads: "A Summary of the various works proposed and executed on the Osborne Estate from 1841 to 1861 inclusive, by direction of HRH the Prince Consort. With continuation to the end of 1879."

A measure of Prince Albert's energy and enthusiasm may be gained from some of the extracts for the year 1846. In this year the Pavilion was finished, Barton Manor rebuilt, and an ice well and the brick arch sewer from the house to the sea were constructed. In addition, 621 500 drain tiles were made, and between 50 and 60 acres were drained in different parts of the estate. The Prince laid out the great belt plantation from the nursery to the Barton Gate, and settled with Mr Dowbiggin for the whole furnishings of the new House, Barton, and the Cottage. At the same time he made plans for further building, including the Terrace of Pavilion and a carriage house.

An insight into the family atmosphere at Osborne may be gained from these further extracts:

October 1850:	The royal children's gardens begun and planted.
6 May 1853:	The royal children lay the first stone of their Swiss Cottage in their gardens.
24 May 1854:	The royal children have the Swiss Cottage given over to them.

3   Halcyon Days

How happy we are here!

On the wall of the dining room at Osborne is a picture by the royal family's favourite artist, Winterhalter, which probably portrays Victoria at the happiest moments of her life. She is represented here with her first five children and the Prince Consort. So far she had not gone through all her regular years of begrudged pregnancies, as she had done when she was photographed with her final family of nine children on the terrace at Osborne. The background of the painting could be anywhere, but as a view of the sea is included it is probable that Winterhalter had in mind one of those happy days at Osborne. The young Princesses Vicky and Alice hover like little birds over baby Princess Helena. The Prince Consort, not looking very comfortable in his court dress, raises his hand to check Affie, who may be toddling too fast. The Queen affectionately holds the Prince of Wales. As yet no discord had come between him and his parents.

Here at Osborne Victoria and Albert felt that they could behave like so many of their subjects, concerned as much as possible with their private affairs and family life. In this environment the Queen was prone to be less irritable. On 29 July 1848 the Hon Eleanor Stanley wrote:

> Last night we had a game of whist, not a rubber, as it was very late . . .; we cut for partners, and the Prince and Queen played together, and the Prince once scolded her abominably for trumping his best spade, but she took it very sweetly, and only laughed, and said she was always afraid of playing with him because he always scolded her. . . .

Lady Lyttleton records an incident two years later:

> Last evening *such* a sunset! I was sitting gazing at it . . . when from an open window below this floor began suddenly to sound the Prince's *orgue expressif* played by his masterly hand. Such a modulation, minor and solemn, and ever changing, and never ceasing, from the piano . . . up to the fullest swell. . . . And it came in so exactly as an accompaniment to the sunset . . . then he went to cut jokes and eat loads of dinner. . . .

The family was never happier, never closer, than at Osborne, where Prince Albert, in his own words, was "partly forester, partly builder, partly farmer and partly gardener." "How happy we are here!" the Queen exclaimed.

As Albert wrote in 1850, "In our island home we are wholly given up to the enjoyment of the warm summer weather. The children catch butterflies,

Victoria sits under the trees." After a fortnight they would return to town. "God be merciful unto us miserable sinners," he finally added. No wonder both parents were more relaxed at Osborne than anywhere else. They heard the voices of their own children, "Such merry voices sounding from all over the lawn at my windows . . . a pretty sight to think of."

One must not think, however, that life at Osborne was spent by Victoria and Albert just sitting under the trees and watching the children chase butterflies. Matters of state arrived almost every day, and Albert was always busy directing the development of the estate. Even so, by no means all the Consort's energies were given to supervising work there. He also supervised Mr William Dyce RA (Superintendent of the School of Design), who was engaged to paint the staircase. The subject was Neptune resigning his Empire to Britannia. Mr Dyce was described by Lady Lyttleton as "one of the least agreeable and most dry and half-sneering mannered men I have ever met," but whatever his manner was, his work was much admired.

At this time Albert wrote to Peel with news of his latest purchases of pictures, on which he had spent £500. The Prince's own room contained paintings of the old school of Italian masters, from Duccio to Lorenzo di Credi. He also bought for his private enjoyment a Cranach triptych. These paintings are no longer at Osborne but are in the royal collection elsewhere.

We can see the Prince in action in a letter from Eleanor Stanley, dated April 1848:

> Just as Lady Canning and I were quietly settled in our drawing room after breakfast, in walked the Prince to see how our rooms were arranged for the third time and to look at what spaces there were for pictures; we consulted with him for two hours or more, running up and down stairs, measuring panels, and discussing the respective merits of the different pictures. He walked into all our rooms, going however through the ceremony of asking our leave; and looking at all our arrangements, and on the whole very agreeable, seeming so pleased. . . .

It must have taken the ladies of the Court by surprise to see the Prince pushing a piano and tables about to see how they looked best.

Among his ever-growing interests Albert constructed a model farm, in which was a cowhouse with a gabled end in the form of a little dog begging and windows of stained glass. It was here, too, at Osborne that Albert could try to improve the sanitation, the defects of which at Windsor and Buckingham Palace had so upset the Queen. Albert's experiment was devised with the help of Dr Lyon Playfair FRS, later President of the Chemical Society. He wrote to Baron Stockmar, his former tutor and secretary, now retired, thinking that he had made an important discovery in turning sewage into agricultural manure.

16

THE ROYAL FAMILY IN 1846

Left to right, Prince Alfred, the Prince of Wales, Queen Victoria, Prince Albert, Princess Alice, Princess Helena and the Princess Royal

(Winterhalter)

However ingenious the principle, the experiment failed at Osborne, apparently because of the lie of the land.

In 1859 the Prince drew up plans for rebuilding the church of St Mildred at Whippingham, and also for a new school there. The existing church was demolished, the materials being used to erect a replacement to the Prince's designs. In May 1860 the Queen and the Prince laid the first stone of the new church, which was completed by the end of 1861. An impressive marble memorial erected by the Queen recalls the death of Prince Albert on 14 December that year at the age of 43.

It was while Albert was watching with an appraising eye the erection of the new church that an unexpected danger beset him. Lord Ernle, then a schoolboy, hid behind a gravestone and took aim with a catapult at an enormously fat foreman, against whom he had a grudge. The Prince, clad in plaid trousers, had mounted the scaffolding with the rector. The bolt went wide, and Albert was the victim. He uttered a loud cry, leapt into the air, and fell backward, being only saved from falling by the other two men. Lord Ernle made good his escape.

Naturally the weather was not always fine—Victoria referred one year to a very cold spring—but on the whole her diaries and letters described blue skies and seas, breakfast in the summer house, sketching with her drawing master Mr Leitch, or a stroll with her husband to view the new plantations, and in the summer to pick strawberries until eight o'clock at night. When the weather was warm they could, from their sitting room balcony, gaze out to sea at the lights of the naval vessels in the Solent. In the grounds they could listen to the nightingales when the birds were in song. The Queen spoke of "the happy peaceful walks he used to take . . . in the woods, and whistling to them [the nightingales] in their own long, peculiar note, which they invariably answered." The Prince was an excellent skater, and in winter there was the lake at Barton on which the family could skate, before spring came round again and there were violets and primroses to pick.

Of course the chief attraction was the beach. Matters had been so arranged that spying eyes from passing boats did not pry into such intimate details as undressing and entering the water. A charming tiled summerhouse in the Italian style was at one end, and there was probably a beach house where the family had tea. The Queen herself was fond of bathing; she records in her diary:

> Drove down to the beach with my maid and went into a bathing machine, where I undressed and bathed in the sea (for the first time in my life) where a very nice woman attended me. I thought it was delightful until I put my head under water, when I thought I would be stifled.

The bathing machine which the Queen used was long left neglected on the beach, but some sixty years ago it was salvaged by the Ministry of Works. On being moved its wheels fell to pieces, but it was carefully reconstructed, and is now housed on a site near the Swiss Cottage.

Osborne proved a valuable haven at times when Queen Victoria went through her periods of depression after childbirth. In 1848, after the birth of Princess Louise and the violent outbreak of the Chartist riots in London, her ministers advised her to flee to Osborne to forget her fears and troubles. The quiet glades of Osborne, however, were made disagreeable by an invasion of toads, and there was a rumour of an attack by forty Chartists who had arrived at Cowes. Cubitt's men, armed with sticks, were mobilised to dispel the raiders, but the threat to the Queen turned out to be as harmless as the toads. They comprised a party of Oddfellows on a Whitsun outing.

Despite this alarm, it was a relief to go to Osborne with the new baby Princess Louise, and forget tiresome politics. Albert, too, found consolation in domesticity. Eleanor Stanley observed:

> The whole Royal family, children, Queen and all, seem to be out the whole day long: I don't believe the Queen thinks of reading a despatch or of doing anything in the way of business, further than scribbling her name where it is required . . . she told Lady C[anning] "she had not read out of a book since February"—she draws a good deal, and walks about and enjoys herself. The children dine and tea in the garden, and run about to their heart's content, and yesterday evening they, assisted by their august Papa, and sanctioned by the presence of their royal Mama, who was looking on, washed a basketful of potatoes and shelled a ditto of peas, which they are to cook for themselves to-day if they are good. Did you ever hear of such happy children?

Although on this one occasion the ministers had recommended Osborne, the house continued to be regarded as a perpetual nuisance for keeping the Queen out of the capital.

In 1852 Napoleon III, who had been elected President of the French Republic on the abdication of Louis Philippe in 1848, named himself Emperor, with his wife Eugénie Empress. It was at Osborne that she and Victoria struck up an intimacy which was to last all their lives. The visit of the Emperor and Empress was made in August 1857, during the yachting season, when the island was more likely to be fashionable and full of visitors. At the time the Anglo–French alliance was on the verge of collapse, and during the four-day visit to what the Queen called "dear modest unpretentious Osborne" the political situation might be saved. A dance was held in the marquee on the lawn, and there were a couple of large dinner parties. The Imperial pair surveyed Albert's model farm, visited Carisbrooke Castle, sailed in the Solent, and drove to Ryde to fill up the programme. They much admired "our dear little pet" Princess Beatrice. The weather was the least admirable, for it was a bad summer with grey skies and sharp showers.

The Empress could not have behaved with greater tact. "She really is quite charming, so lovely, so graceful, so merry, so natural, clever and lively and full of conversation," commented the Queen. Eugénie, with great discretion, avoided the Queen's uncomfortable breakfasts, when windows were kept open no matter what the weather was. She made a late entry in her exquisite pastel-coloured dresses, and the day, other than when driving, was spent chatting or walking with the children. There was the usual planting of a tree, and then Albert and Napoleon had their political talk, after which the royal party separated to dress for dinner. In a white organdie crinoline, and with flowers in her hair, Eugénie enlivened the conversation with her cleverness and originality. Here I should mention that they indulged in the then popular pastime of table-tapping—for amusement, of course; but the records do not say how successful they were.

The Imperial couple left after the usual exchange of gifts, and on this occasion with floods of tears. The children, described as "*les plus charmants enfants*," were declared by the Queen as quite adoring the Empress. All boarded the royal yacht *La Reine Hortense* to see them off, after which Albert and Victoria returned rather "*désoeuvrés*." The yacht finally sailed away to the cries of the French sailors: "*Vive la reine d'Angleterre.*"

4 The Prince Consort and the Royal Children

Children, though often a source of anxiety and difficulty, are a great blessing and cheer and brighten up life

One day while walking in the grounds at Osborne, Albert pointed to the trees which he had planted, and remarked to his wife: "I shall never see these grow up." Victoria asked him, "Why not? You will be only sixty, and that is not very old." "No," he repeated, "I shall never see them grow up."

On the Queen's birthday in 1852, in spite of his depression, the Prince planted new gardens. The lime and the oranges, with their strong smell, reminded him of Gotha.

In August 1854 the Queen noted:

> . . . the birthday of my beloved husband, . . . we celebrated peacefully and happily in the bosom of our family [at Osborne]. The children did all they could to make their dear adored father happy; they drew, worked, recited, wrote compositions, played on the piano and Affie the violin.

It was probably three years after this that the only known photograph of the complete royal family was taken, on the terrace at Osborne House. It has been reproduced in engravings many times, and it forms a striking contrast to the 1848 painting by Winterhalter. The Queen is seated with the youngest child, Princess Beatrice, on her lap, and standing behind her is the Princess Royal. She was described as "very nervy." At seventeen years of age she was to marry the Crown Prince of Prussia and leave home for a long time. Although the parents were pleased at the match, the Consort suffered further depression at the thought of losing her. (Shortly after the photograph was taken, Vicky left England, though she continued to visit Osborne whenever she could.) On the right of the photograph stands the Prince of Wales, in the gawky stage of early youth. He was still under the rule of tutors and closely watched by his father. Beside the Queen stand the two younger children. The Consort, looking somewhat stouter and balder than in earlier pictures, stands scarcely looking at his children or his wife, whose eye half glances at him.

The Prince spent long hours planning his children's education. And whether the royal family happened to be at Windsor, Balmoral, or Osborne, their routine of work and play was carefully supervised by the Prince himself. On educational matters he was in many ways in advance of his time, but

THE ROYAL FAMILY AT OSBORNE IN MAY 1857

Left to right, Prince Alfred, Prince Albert, Princess Alice, Queen Victoria and Princess
Helena, Prince Arthur, Princess Louise, Prince Leopold, Princess Beatrice, the Princess Royal, the Prince of Wales (later Edward VII)

THE SWISS COTTAGE

unfortunately he was all at sea when he dealt with his own children, and with no one more than the poor little stuttering Prince of Wales, who was thought by both parents to be very backward, and not a bit clever like Vicky, who was her father's favourite. At Osborne, as elsewhere, the Prince of Wales was accompanied by Mr Gibbs, his tutor, who had little understanding of a boy's mind. The family enjoyed delightful picnics at the rock springs at Ventnor or trips to Bonchurch, but often the Prince of Wales and Prince Alfred had to continue their studies instead. In the evening the children had to take part in charades, often sketched by their loving parents. Even then, such enjoyment could be marred by having to memorise speeches by Racine.

Although Osborne was a holiday home, the daily life there was spartan. The meals were simple indeed: a bit of roast meat and perhaps a plain pudding. The princesses were taught to be careful and tidy with their clothing: kid gloves, after being worn, had to be blown out so that the fingers would not lose their shape; bonnet ribbons had to be neatly rolled so that they would appear uncreased when next used; and ribbons from the Queen's discarded hats were ironed and handed on to tie around the brims of the children's hats.

Princess Louise was rather shy and retiring but soon began to show signs of artistic gifts—strangely enough, for that period, in sculpture. Specimens of her work may still be seen at Osborne. Alfred (Affie) had a naval career planned for him, but the wretched Prince of Wales, contented himself, like Traddles in *David Copperfield*, with drawing—not, however, skeletons, but army uniforms, an interest that lasted him all his life. Arthur, his mother's favourite, was happy with his toy soldiers. Leopold was intelligent, but temperamental, and early showed signs of having the dreaded haemophilia, though he lived to maturity and fathered two children.

Snow was one of the few excuses for closing books at Osborne. The Prince Consort, in particular, liked the snow because it reminded him of his native home. The children were taught to skate on the lake at Barton Manor, and sometimes were allowed to build large snowballs. In one hard winter they made a big snowman with a carrot nose, black eyes, and an old hat on his head.

In 1854 an important step was taken to give the family greater privacy and more opportunities for the practical education of the children. Already small gardens had been started for each of them, and each child was equipped with little garden tools that bore the names of the owners. The new feature was a chalet, which was prefabricated in Switzerland and comprises, with its external gallery and staircase, and carved German psalms and proverbs, the sort of house that could have come from the pages of Grimm. On the ground floor the little girls learned to cook and serve simple dishes, using the bright copper utensils and charming Wedgwood china. Upstairs there was simple but no less charming furniture of light wood, and a cradle in which the youngest could sleep during the day. A small dog-cart or pony-trap took the family down to the chalet, and there, and on the beach, they could enjoy a time of freedom and privacy that must have seemed only too short.

Albert, an expert carpenter and mechanic, passed his skills on to the boys in a little workshop installed in the Swiss Cottage. When one of the children produced a good vegetable plot the under-gardener was instructed to present a certificate; this was handed to Papa, who then bought the produce at the current market price. Nearby Prince Arthur constructed a miniature fort.

The children were taught to swim in a floating bath in the bay, devised by Papa, who also showed them how to fly kites. "He plays with them so delightfully," the Queen noted in her journal. She could not bring herself to do so with the same joyous abandon. In that relaxed atmosphere the once demure, backward little Alice became—according to her governess—"as wild as a fawn." No wonder that years later Princess Alice regarded her days at Swiss Cottage as among the happiest in her life, and the Prince of Wales, visiting Osborne in 1872 after a serious illness, wept when he saw again his little wheelbarrow and spade.

The children had a natural history museum of their own, and on their walks were instructed by their father to collect every item that might be of geological or botanical interest. Through the years, by the efforts of so many children, supplemented by gifts from home and abroad, a great number and strange variety of objects were deposited there and may be seen there now. Other entertainments were unwittingly provided by visiting Ojibwa Indians, by a Chinaman with two dwarf small-footed wives, and by three Highland dwarfs, two of them, brother and sister, being only forty-four inches high.

The influence of Baron Stockmar was to be seen in the bringing up of the girls as well as of the boys. It was he who recommended that the princesses should be taught to be efficient women, capable of running a home, and acting as seamstresses and embroiderers. Sometimes the Queen and the Prince would dine at the cottage, so that they might see for themselves what progress their daughters were making. Occasionally the girls would bake for the sick folk in the neighbourhood, but in later years their most regular order was for export. Each week they cooked a batch of cakes and pies for Princess Victoria, by then married to Prince Frederick William, son of the Prussian King. These strange parcels would arrive from Osborne in the hands of the Queen's Messenger, with more conventional packages.

On the occasion of the eighteenth anniversary of her wedding, in February 1858, the Queen was able to write, from the high peak of her happiness:

> [Albert] has brought such universal blessings on this country and Europe! For *what* has not my beloved and perfect Albert done? Raised monarchy to the *highest* pinnacle of *respect*, and rendered it *popular* beyond what it *ever* was in this country!

Later that year there was joy for the Queen and Prince when they returned to Osborne, to find Affie on the wharf in his midshipman's jacket and cap. He had passed his examinations with some credit.

When the Queen celebrated her birthday in May 1860 she felt that such happiness must go on for ever. Even her old mother, the Duchess of Kent, in spite of severe pain and illness, was with her. In a letter to Princess Augusta of Prussia the Queen paid a moving tribute to her husband:

> Where could I point to another woman who after 20 years of such marital felicity still possesses it? My dearly-beloved Albert shows me not only as much affection and kindness as ever, but as much love and tenderness as on the first day of our marriage. How can I ever repay him for it?

The weather was exceptionally fine, and nightingales sang "all round the house." Musicians played on the terrace, and there was dancing and merriment as there had been nine years before.

Changes had, however, taken place in those nine years. Mention has already been made of the marriage of seventeen-year-old Vicky to Prince Frederick William of Prussia. The Prince of Wales had quitted the schoolroom for Oxford, but he was guarded and supervised as much as ever. Prince Alfred was beginning to show promise in his training as a naval officer. But Albert remained depressed. He wrote moodily to his daughter Vicky comparing himself to the donkey at the well of Carisbrooke Castle, his true counterpart, "who would rather munch thistles in the Castle Moat, . . . small are the thanks he gets for his labour."

In July to October 1860 the Prince of Wales visited Canada and the United States. His tour was a success, and he proved a popular figure wherever he went. Nevertheless his conduct was causing his parents much anxiety. The engagement of Princess Alice to Prince Louis of Hesse-Darmstadt, late in 1860, was marred for the Queen by gossip concerning the Prince of Wales and a Dublin actress.

The year 1861 was a sad and tragic one for the Queen, at the end of which it seemed that all happiness had gone and nothing but worry confronted her. The Duchess of Kent died after a painful illness, an event which both the Queen and her husband felt deeply. They returned to Osborne in June, only to find little Prince Leopold, the delicate haemophiliac child, so ill with measles that he had to be sent to the south of France for his health. One woe trod upon another's heels, for Albert lost a much-loved cousin who died of typhoid. The Prince, however, unknown to most, was the real cause of anxiety. Even the Queen wrote to her daughter at a time when Albert had a bad cold: "Dear Papa never allows he is getting over it, but makes such a miserable face that people always believe he is very ill." Only Stockmar warned that Albert would never fight for life if he were ill.

26

The Prince Consort exhausted himself, not only in attending various meetings, but in visiting his son at Cambridge (where the Prince had gone from Oxford in January 1861), and also in the delicate task of avoiding British intervention in the American Civil War.

That year the Queen's birthday was again spent at Osborne, but with the death of the Duchess of Kent on his mind Albert merely pottered about the gardens and read a few novels, a pursuit completely alien to his nature. In November the illness that had puzzled his physicians began to show itself. At first the Queen was unaware of its seriousness, but when it dawned on her she was driven almost demented with worry. She was ill-prepared to cope when he died of typhoid at Windsor on 14 December 1861.

Stunned with grief, and on the verge of what was obviously a nervous breakdown, the Queen was advised by King Leopold, in spite of protests from Princess Alice, to go at once to Osborne, without waiting for the funeral. Having selected a site at Frogmore (Windsor) for a family mausoleum for Albert and herself, she returned to East Cowes four days later, a pathetic little figure in black. It was a very tempestuous night and the boat rocked as she landed. To help her ashore she needed the assistance of the Duchess of Atholl, who had travelled with her, and who wrote later to Lady Biddulph, wife of the Master of the Household:

> I have not yet recovered [from] the *desolate* look on that young face in Her *Widow's* cap! for somehow the Queen looked like a *child*—And then her passionate embrace!—I felt—*what* was there I would not do for her!

Her step-brother Ernest met her on the stairs at Osborne, and the two wept together as the storm broke against the windows. Shortly afterwards she was joined by her children, and from then on she continued her regular migrations to her three homes, but without *him*.

Numb with shock, the Queen discontinued her diary. Instead she wrote numerous letters on mourning paper with wide black margins. To her uncle Leopold she wrote of herself:

> The poor fatherless baby of eight months is now the utterly broken-hearted and crushed widow of forty-two! My *life* as a *happy* one is *ended*! the world is gone for *me*! If I *must live* on . . . it is from henceforth for our poor fatherless children—for my unhappy country, which has lost *all* in losing him.

Clearly she thought that grief would destroy her when she wrote: "It is but for a short time, and *then* I go, *never, never*, to part!"

With this in mind, the Queen hurried back to Frogmore to make sure that the mausoleum was being built according to her plans. But she soon returned again to the island. Looking out at Osborne on the frost-covered landscape she could have cried out with Cleopatra of Egypt that there was nothing left remarkable beneath the visiting moon. "There is nobody to call.me Victoria now. The things of this life are of no interest to the Queen." She pondered deeply about death and reunion with her husband. She wrote at this time to Lord Canning, who had just lost his wife:

> To the Queen it is like *death* in life! . . . she feels *alone* in the wide world, with many helpless children . . . to look to her . . . *now* when she can barely struggle with her wretched existence! . . . her utter despair—she *cannot* describe! Her only support—the only ray of comfort she gets for *a moment*, is in the *firm conviction* and certainty of his nearness, his undying love, and of their eternal reunion!

During the time she was at Osborne a note of determination, almost of defiance, crept into the Queen's correspondence. If she was to live on, not to die, then she would make sure that her hero, her gloriously great husband, the life and soul of everything, should not be forgotten; all his dearest wishes should be carried out.

The same ritual was carried out at Osborne as at Balmoral and Windsor; Albert's clothes and a jug of hot water and a clean towel were placed in his dressing-room at night. For some years she slept clasping Albert's nightshirt in her arms. Visitors to Osborne can still see the pocket for his watch, and the picture of the Prince lying in state like a gallant knight. These relics, and a wreath of immortelles, remained by the Queen's bed during her lifetime.

"I will, I will do my duty," she often repeated to herself as she toiled away without Albert's help. She complained often that she was seldom in bed before twelve o'clock. At Osborne she avoided the prying eyes of intruders. If anyone other than her children came near her, they were her ladies, who were widows like herself.

Princess Alice, who was so good to her and had acted for the time as her secretary, was to be married in July 1862. The marriage had been agreed on before the death of the Prince Consort, and it was felt that it could not be postponed any longer. Prince Louis of Hesse duly arrived at Osborne overjoyed at the prospect of his marriage. The Queen slept little on the night before the wedding. Alice went to see her mother on the wedding morning, and she received from her, as Vicky had done before her, a prayer book. They breakfasted together and went to look at the dining room which had been converted into a chapel. The family picture by Winterhalter had been placed over the altar. The guests were to breakfast in the Council Chamber, apart from the Queen.

Only relatives had been invited: Louis' two brothers and his father the Grand Duke, Ernest of Saxe-Coburg-Gotha, Prince Augustus of Saxe-Coburg-Kohary, Princess Feodora Hohenlohe (the Queen's half-sister), and Crown Prince

Frederick of Prussia (Fritz). Vicky, who was expecting the birth of her second son, Henry, was prevented from attending this important family event.

Alice was dressed in a wedding gown and veil of Honiton lace, made after a pattern designed by her late father. The Princesses Helena, Louise, and Beatrice wore similar veils. A somewhat ghostly silence prevailed as the uneasy guests did not quite know how to behave. The Queen was led in, flanked by her four sons, and took her seat in an armchair close to the altar, so that no one could see her face. The men wore black evening coats, white waistcoats, and grey trousers; the ladies wore grey or violet mourning dresses. Ernest of Saxe-Coburg-Gotha gave the bride away. The service was read by the Archbishop of York, who read it with tears running down his face, for he had lost his wife four years before. Affie, always emotional, sobbed all through the service, and afterwards most dreadfully. The Queen broke down too, as she embraced the bridal pair, retiring with them and Princess Beatrice to the Horn Room. Seated together thus, the Queen wearing—as Princess Beatrice called it—"Ma's sad cap," the lunch recalled Hamlet's remark that "the funeral bak'd meats did coldly furnish forth the marriage table."

After the Queen had left the bride and bridegroom, to go upstairs, they went into the Council Chamber, where they met the other guests. Princess Alice and her husband then left quietly for their honeymoon, the first part of which was spent at "St Clare," near Ryde, then they spent a short time on the Continent.

As a consolation for her mother, Alice promised to return home in the autumn. Princess Charles, Alice's mother-in-law, jibbed at this. Queen Victoria thought she was most unamiable. Louis was more understanding. Alice, who had dedicated her life to looking after her dear mama after the death of her father, took a firm stand with her husband's relations; and Queen Victoria, whatever her mental state, was determined to rule her daughter's affairs and to ride roughshod over in-laws.

The Prince of Wales came of age in 1862. He had never felt at home at Osborne. Barton Manor had been bought with him in mind, but he looked forward to being far away, in Sandringham. The Prince had fixed his eyes on the lovely Princess Alexandra of Denmark. She was invited to stay with the Queen at Osborne in November 1862. The gentle princess received constant warnings about the behaviour of the Prince of Wales, which she accepted without comment. This was probably the right attitude, for the Queen said to Lady Bruce later that Alexandra was a jewel dropped from the skies, and that "she would act right fearlessly and *would not knuckle under*." The marriage, in March 1863, was a success in spite of the Queen's fears, and before long the Prince of Wales and his bride were able to welcome distinguished guests on the steps of the Royal Yacht Squadron.

Three years later there was another wedding: Princess Helena married Prince Christian of Schleswig-Holstein.

5 The Two Comforters and an Old Friend

"Friend more than servant." He [Lord Tennyson] was very sympathising to me, quite remarkably so

Two persons came into Queen Victoria's life during her long period of mourning at Osborne house. In their own unique way they gave her the consolation and mental stability she needed at the time. One was the simple, brusque Highlander John Brown, and the other the highly popular yet unaffected Poet Laureate, Alfred Tennyson.

Prior to John Brown's arrival the Queen had written a letter to her favourite friend Lady Augusta Bruce: "My only desire is to continue as he my beloved angel could have wished—and yet I know and feel how many things—how many relationships have altered, and I must find consolation where I can."

As if in answer to this prayer John Brown arrived at Osborne from Balmoral on a very cold day in December 1864. He brought with him jars of homemade jam and a dozen egg cups, one of which was used by the Queen at breakfast time every Sunday. He brought with him also Victoria's favourite pony, Lochnagar. On her ponies he subsequently led her about, talking quietly, always attentive and cheerful, and very quickly became known at Osborne as "the Queen's Highland servant."

Dependable he may have been, but members of the Court and the staff found him coarse and commonplace. The quiet countryfolk at East Cowes thought his manner of speaking to his sovereign as "wumman," telling her to hold her head up while he fastened her scarf, and giving her advice about her clothes, as impudent beyond all bounds. I have met several old people at East Cowes who have told me of the strong dislike which their grandparents had for this worthy Scotsman.

The Queen's favour undoubtedly turned his head, and he had the unfortunate habit of rephrasing, to inferiors and superiors alike, his own interpretation of the Queen's commands and replies to messages. At Osborne there were plenty of examples of this. On one occasion he snubbed the Prime Minister, Gladstone, who had been invited to dine with the Queen; he touched him on the back at table and said sharply: "Ye've talked enough." No doubt the Queen was grateful, though she may not have said so; for her minister was a slow eater, but a lengthy talker, while she ate fast and disliked talk at mealtimes.

When the Mayor of Portsmouth called in 1869 to invite the Queen to attend the Volunteer Review, the message was given to Brown, who should have passed it on to the private secretary to deliver and return a reply. Brown typically took upon himself both duties. He went away with the message, only to push his head inside the door a few moments later with the curt answer: "The Queen says, 'saretenly not.' " Crestfallen and humiliated, the mayor had to withdraw.

Henry Ponsonby, the most human and kindly of the Queen's secretaries, had on another occasion to patch up a sharp quarrel between Prince Alfred and Brown. Ponsonby was also involved when one of the Queen's sons-in-law, having gone out early one morning to shoot pheasants, complained to him that Brown had been out before him and had shot all the available birds.

King Edward VII destroyed most of the memorials which were scattered with considerable liberality by the Queen when unexpectedly in 1883 her faithful henchman died; but the memorial at Osborne escaped and can still be seen bearing an inscription which Tennyson found from Lord Byron.

The most interesting relic of Brown at Osborne, however, is the famous painting of the Queen reading her dispatches on the back of her horse Flora. The artist, Landseer, was ageing at the time, and his sight was beginning to fail. The horse, dogs, and other details are painted with his old brilliance, but the painting of Osborne appears more like the back-drop of a stage scene than anything else. On a seat nearby are the Princesses Louise and Helena. What caused most amusement was not the unlikely act of the Queen reading her dispatches on horseback, but Brown himself, partly, apparently, because he wore an unauthentic black tartan, and partly because he was depicted with a pointed beard. Although the Queen had taken considerable trouble to send the artist a photograph of Brown's face and fringe of beard, Landseer was too old to alter his picture. When it was exhibited at the Royal Academy it drew from *Punch* the comment: "All is black that is not brown."

A bagpipe factory was apparently established at East Cowes while Brown was at Osborne, but I am sure that this was not in his honour. The Queen had always a piper with her, and he used to play on the lawn every morning before breakfast.

One cannot pass by an object which is irreverently known as "Vicky's ticker." Until 1963 there was exhibited in a glass case in the College of Psychic Science, London, a gold watch which has since been stolen. The first of two inscriptions on the back apparently read: "To Miss Georgiana Eagle for her Meritorious & Extraordinary Clairvoyance produced at Osborn House [note the misspelling] in the Isle of Wight July 15th 1846." The second inscription indicated that the watch was given to a Mrs Etta Wreidt.

There is no doubt that the Queen was at this time deeply interested in the question of life after death. Brown, like so many Highlanders, was supposed to be gifted with second sight, and doubtless the Queen often talked to him on the subject. While at Balmoral, Brown learnt in a more practical way about the spirit world. He would pour a dram of whisky into his mistress's afternoon teapot. He thought this would put "spurrit into the pur wumman." The custom continued with Brown thereafter wherever he went. Whether the Queen really enjoyed the beverage is very uncertain. At that time she was willing to accept meekly and without comment whatever Brown did. Like Sterne's Uncle Toby, she was unable to "stop the mouth of a faithful servant." And so whenever the Royal Standard fluttered from the masthead at Osborne, everyone knew that Brown was about, and minded his or her Ps and Qs accordingly.

Like John Brown, Tennyson met the Prince Consort during the last few years of his life. In 1850 Wordsworth died, and Tennyson was made Poet Laureate. He married in the same year, and after a period in which his reputation both as a poet and as an outspoken political writer gradually rose, the Tennyson family rented "Farringford," some 15 miles from Osborne House. Continued success with his new poem *In Memoriam* encouraged him to buy the place. By 1856 he had two boys, Hallam and Lionel, aged four and two. On 13 May of that year the Prince Consort called at Farringford, and the episode is described in Emily Tennyson's diary:

> In the midst of all our confusion while all imaginable things strewed the drawing room and the bookshelves were bare and the chairs and tables dancing Prince Albert came. He had driven over suddenly from Osborne. . . . One of the gentlemen with the Prince gathered a large bunch of cowslips which the Prince said he must take himself and give to the Queen. One dropt and I kept it for the children as a memorial. A nightingale was singing while he was here. . . .

The Prince said on leaving Farringford: "It is such a pretty place that I shall certainly bring the Queen to see it." Owing to a series of unforeseen circumstances the visit was deferred. Soon after this, Tennyson embarked upon his second major work, which greatly influenced the Queen, *The Idylls of the King.* At the Prince's personal request, a copy was sent to the royal library at Windsor.

When the Prince Consort died the Tennysons lost no time in driving to Osborne to sign the visitors' book, and Alfred set to work at once writing his memorial dedication to Prince Albert for a new edition of *The Idylls of the King.* It was a favourite poem of the Queen, who often used the misquoted line: "Wearing *the lily* of a blameless life."

In April 1862, when Hallam was aged nine and Lionel eight, Tennyson was invited to have his first personal introduction to the Queen. The meeting is briefly recorded by the Queen: "I went down to see Tennyson who is very peculiar looking, tall, dark, with a fine head . . . I told him how much I admired his glorious lines to my precious Albert and how much comfort I found in his

32

In Memoriam. . . . When he spoke of my own loss, of that to the Nation, his eyes quite filled with tears."

From Osborne, on 14 January 1863, Tennyson received a specially bound volume of *The Principal Speeches and Addresses of His Royal Highness the Prince Consort*. On the title page was written: "To Alfred Tennyson Esquire who so truly appreciated this greatest purest and best of men from the beloved Prince's broken-hearted widow Victoria. Osborne Dec. 9, 1862." In reply, Tennyson wrote in *The Times* his fine poem on the engagement of the Prince of Wales to Alexandra of Denmark.

Another meeting between the Queen and the Poet Laureate, at Osborne in May 1863, is best described by ten-year-old Hallam Tennyson, with his naive candour and his reference to the royal children, who were about his age. The two boys visited Swiss Cottage, with an old dame of 81 in it. They saw the model shop, which visitors can still see, and the little fort that Prince Arthur constructed with handmade bricks:

> . . . with a very little help. It was called Victoria fort and Albert barracks. . . . Prince Arthur is destined for an engineer. . . . We drove back to Osborne. We went into one of the drawing-rooms. . . . I had a chat with Prince Leopold about the South of France and Paris, he said he did not like Boulogne. The Princess Louisa asked me whether I could draw, I told her I could not. She can draw beautifully. . . . Prince Leopold . . . talked about his fine ships, . . . he talks of building castles in this quiet part of the sea. . . .
>
> The Queen wears a locket round her neck with thin black velvet. The Queen is not stout. Her Majesty has a large mind and a small body to contain it therein. We went into Lady Augusta's room and had tea. We saw Sir Charles Phipps, the Secretary to the Queen. . . . We saw Prince Alfred, he looked just like a Norwegian. He shook hands with Papa and was very reverential to him. . . . We saw Prince Louis of Hesse. . . . Her Majesty has a beautiful little nose and soft blue eyes. . . . List of Princes and Princesses . . . in the order we saw them, Prince Alfred, Prince Louis of Hesse, Princess Alice, Princess Helena, Princess Beatrice, Princess Louisa, Prince Leopold. . . .
>
> *Observations:* You must always say "Mam" when in her Majesty's presence. You must stand until the Queen asks you to sit down. Her Majesty does not often tell you to sit down. . . .

For some time after this the Tennysons saw little of the Queen; the poet's close association with his "dear and honoured lady" did not begin until after the death of John Brown, of erysipelas, in 1883. This was a great blow to the Queen, but by bringing her in touch again with Lord Tennyson it gave her fresh opportunities to discuss life after death. Tennyson still retained Farringford, but publicity and the inquisitiveness of the public had forced him to retreat to Haslemere, where he had bought a house. After Brown's death he travelled to the island to see the Queen, who wrote of the event in her diary:

> [I] saw the great Poet *Tennyson* in dearest Albert's room for nearly an hour . . . He is grown very old—his eyesight much impaired and he is very shaky on his legs. But he was very kind. Asked him to sit down.

Naturally the Queen talked of her love for *In Memoriam* and of what the poem meant to her. Next year she sent to him a copy of *More Leaves from a Journal of our Life in the Highlands* inscribed "by a very humble and unpretending author."

The death in that year, 1884, of the Queen's "dearest of dear sons," Prince Leopold, brought from Tennyson a short ode, ending:

> Oh Mother-Queen, and weeping Wife
> The Death, for which you mourn, is Life!

He was less successful with an ode on the marriage of Princess Beatrice in 1885, and the Princess herself understandably objected to the lines:

> The Mother weeps
> At that white funeral of the single life.

Another friend whose friendship reawakened after a lapse of a good many years was the Empress Eugénie. During what the Queen called "this dreadful year," 1871, the Prince Imperial fled to England. He landed at Hastings, to be joined later by his parents. Napoleon III died at Chislehurst in 1873, and the Prince joined the British Army; he was killed six years later in the Zulu War. With the death of her husband and son Eugénie she gave up the beautiful pastel frocks she had formerly worn at Osborne, and became a smart business woman, but her friendship with the Queen was as strong as ever. She visited the Queen as often as possible, sometimes living at Kent House; for a time she had an apartment of her own in West Cowes. In contrast to her bourgeois appearance she kept, though she did not wear, diamonds worth some £50 000.

When in the first year of her widowhood the Empress landed quietly at East Cowes, Lord Albemarle wrote of the occasion:

> My cousin, Sir Harry Stephenson, was in waiting. . . . it was bitterly cold day and a persistent drop hung on the end of Harry's nose. As for the Empress, you can imagine her feelings after all she had been through, and her emotion at returning to her old home. When the time came for Harry's obeisance over Her Majesty's lap-gloved hand he deposited on it a drop. This being taken for a tear completed the undoing of the Empress, who burst into tears.

In the manner of the elderly ladies in Arnold Bennett's *The Old Wives' Tale*, Eugénie and the Queen could contemplate the past in their coach drives about the island. They revisited the scenes of early days—Sandrock, Bonchurch, and the Convent of St Clare, where Eugénie knelt and prayed for the souls of her husband and son.

Before the Empress moved to West Cowes her presence at Kent House caused much irritation to the Maids of Honour, who often went over to Kent House, without permission, to talk to their gentleman friends who were sometimes lodged there. The Queen had, unfortunately for them, the habit of arriving unannounced to take the Empress for a drive, and the ladies had to scuttle back to the House, or hide themselves discreetly, until the danger was past.

In 1877 a railway station with the name Whippingham was built on the Ryde–Newport line with a view to serving Osborne. It was, however, some 3 miles from Osborne House, and even as a connection with Ryde it served very little useful purpose. It was used only once by the Queen when she and Eugénie made a tour of the island by train.

6 The Black Queen

For all this I must try to live on for a little while yet

The long wintry period of mourning extended from 1861 to approximately 1871. Most historians agree that during this period Queen Victoria made her worst mistakes as a parent and as a monarch, and the reputation of the throne sank almost as low as it had in the reign of George IV.

Blindly ignoring what her subjects felt, the Queen declined all public engagements, and carried on her set routine, returning to Osborne each year in August and December.

From very early days of her widowhood, Victoria was determined that no one should guide her or dictate to her. To Lord John Russell she sent a sharp reminder that he must keep to the rule that no communications should be sent until she had approved the drafts. Having to bring these drafts by hand to the Isle of Wight increased the irritation ministers felt at her presence at Osborne. When Parliamentary bills were being read for her approval, the Queen usually sat in the small state room (the Audience Room) under the chandelier, with the Clerk to the Privy Council, Sir Arthur Helps. The door was open into the adjoining Council Chamber, where the ministers sat, and the Queen listened to each item of the bills and nodded her assent. Helps then signalled back to the ministers the royal agreement to each item.

A strange meeting took place shortly after the death of the Consort. Lord Palmerston, who had never been a favourite of the Queen or of the Consort, came to Osborne when he heard the news. Seated in the small audience room in her "sad cap," the Queen forgave the old statesman his green gloves, blue studs, and dyed whiskers when he wept openly for her loss.

Family affairs continued to keep the Queen busy. Whenever the children came to Osborne she had to exert herself. Already the tiny feet of her grandchildren were beginning to patter up and down the corridors, while the youngest of her own children still required attention. Vicky, when she came to visit her mother, now brought with her Wilhelm and Charlotte, whom everyone except John Brown appeared to dislike. Young Wilhelm sulked all the way up from the beach one day because he could not ride in the front of the carriage. On the same visit, when the five year old was told to bow to some visitors, a look of proud defiance crept into the boy's eyes; a look that was quickly dispelled when the keen blue eyes of his grandmother grew suddenly very cold, and the young prince bowed very low indeed. Little Princess Charlotte received a sharp rebuke when she refused to shake hands with John Brown, saying that she had been told not to be familiar with servants. In spite of protests

THE ROYAL FAMILY AT OSBORNE ON 19 APRIL 1870
Left to right, Princess Beatrice, Prince Albert Victor of Wales, Prince Leopold, Prince
George of Wales, Princess Louise, Queen Victoria, Princess Louise of Wales,
Alexandra, Princess of Wales

37

she had to carry out Gan-gan's command and shake hands with John Brown.

At last, in 1865, Queen Victoria recovered the will to live and gradually ceased speaking of joining her husband in death. "For all this I must try to live on for a little while yet." It is a pity that she did not make this resolve clear to her country.

In that same year Uncle Leopold died, and Victoria became, as Prince Alice put it, "Head of the Family." This change made Osborne an important gathering centre for her family, for ministers and for other guests.

At this point it seems advisable to describe another person who came to take a leading part in life at Osborne. Henry Ponsonby has already been referred to as a humane and kindly man. In 1861, at the age of 37, he was one of the Consort's equerries, when the Queen took him over in that capacity. He was a Liberal, but never allowed his politics to direct the Queen. From 1865 to 1870, when he became the Queen's private secretary, his witty letters and notes enliven what must have been a very dreary period at Osborne. For the latter part of his life, when not travelling with the Queen, he lived mostly at Kent House in the grounds of Osborne, but the Ponsonby family later moved to Osborne Cottage, where Sir Henry (he was knighted in 1879) died in 1895 of a stroke.

Fortunately for him, Henry Ponsonby, although at this time a Major-General, was not made to present himself with all the impeccable smartness required of an army officer. It was only when the Prince of Wales was about that Ponsonby feared that "he might not mingle well with the white cotton stockings" worn by the footmen at Osborne.

Two examples from later years will show his quality. On one occasion the following exchange of notes took place with Sir William Harcourt:

"Dear Ponsonby, Is it 'knees'? Yrs, W.V.H."

The reply came back:

"Dear Harcourt, As no ladies will be present trousers will be worn, Yrs, H.F.P."

When General De Plat, one of the Queen's equerries, was lodged at Barton Manor, he declared that as he lay in the four-poster bed there he had reached the height of his ambition; he wanted nothing and envied no man.

In the confines of the royal circle Ponsonby moved with remarkable tact and diplomacy. Neither the Queen nor her children were easy to deal with, and as time went on the relationships between them grew more difficult as each child got married. At Osborne, although the Queen expected visits from her children, she never made them welcome.

The Prince of Wales, in particular, taxed Ponsonby's ability to keep him busy and contented. The Queen laid down rules on the day he was to come to Osborne, and decreed that he was to leave it on the day before the Cowes regatta began. "Will the Queen never find out," wrote Ponsonby, "that she will have ten times more influence with her children by treating them with kindness and not trying to rule them like a despot?"

One of many complications in Sir Henry's work was the Queen's preference for cold rooms. Warned one day that the Queen was coming, the Ponsonby family set to to extinguish the drawing room fire with a bucket of water, quickly opening the windows to get rid of the stench.

Such devotion to duty did not always reap its just reward. Victoria's characteristic imperiousness continued throughout her life. She made it a rule that no one was allowed to go out before the Queen. In 1885 it happened that Sir Henry and the private secretary, Major Edwards, went out together. Sir Henry received the following letter from the Queen:

> The Queen *must* ask that both Sir Henry and Major Edwards should *not* be out on Sunday Mrg or any other *at the same time*. Not 5 minutes after the service in the Chapel was over she sent to say she wished to see Sir Henry in a ¼ of an hour but was told he was gone to church. . . .

In spite of what Ponsonby called the Queen's "luxury of woe" she put herself out when the Sultan of Turkey arrived on a state visit in 1867. Although there were squalls and heavy rain she led a review of the fleet off Spithead, and while in the *Victoria and Albert* she invested the Sultan with the Garter. She herself was a good sailor, but the Sultan was seasick, and the ceremony must have been a somewhat comic one. However, the visit went off well, with good wishes on both sides.

The Queen's protests could not prevent political events from crowding in on her. Later in 1867 her life was in some danger by threats from the Fenians. Three of them were hanged in Manchester, and Prince Alfred was shot and wounded by another in Australia. News came from Canada in December that eighty people had started off with murderous intentions against the Queen. The plot was apparently to capture her under the very eyes of John Brown while she was driving on the Osborne estate. The Queen, who was then at Osborne, was vainly besought by Lord Grey to leave the Isle of Wight and go to Windsor for greater security. He angrily announced that unless she listened to him he would wash his hands of her safety, but Victoria retorted that a show of fear was unnecessary. Lord Derby reminded her that long and late drives with even her faithful attendant were risky. The Queen sharply replied that long and late drives did not take place at Osborne.

She flatly refused to escape to London or to Windsor, while complaining that she was no better than a state prisoner. Nearly 200 soldiers, including a contingent of the Life Guards, were moved to the island, and coastal and naval vessels patrolled. Only the Queen's own intervention prevented the arrival of the cavalry. The "attack" ended when an over-assiduous sentry arrested Mr Page, a gamekeeper, who lived at Swiss Cottage, and another sentry arrested

Prince Arthur, who had come to spend Christmas with his mother. "Everyone lost their head," wrote the Queen, forgetting her grammar when she lambasted those concerned for their credulity.

Apart from such events, life went on unaltered, although she was asked by Gladstone in 1869 to leave Osborne a few days earlier than usual in order to open Blackfriars Bridge. After some grumbling she gave way, "but on no account must such a request be made again." All must be reminded that "*his* loss would still darken her world forever."

On the other hand, the marriage of Princess Louise to Lord Lorne, heir to the Duke of Argyll, in 1871, pleased Victoria very much. It served to augment her connection with Scotland. In the island she was inspired to erect a memorial in St Thomas' Church, Newport, to Elizabeth Stuart, daughter of Charles I, who had died in Carisbrooke Castle and was buried in the church. She also inaugurated a fund to reconstruct the chapel of St Nicholas-in-Castro, in the precincts of the castle, in memory of Charles I.

About this time the Queen waltzed, for the first time since her bereavement, with Louise, who continued to add to her artistic sculptures at Osborne. Once again could be heard, after so many years, the little gold bell which called all the family to watch charades, *tableaux vivants*, and theatricals. The Queen attended rehearsals and expected an audience. Princess Beatrice often took a leading part, and ladies of the Court and gentlemen such as Ponsonby were expected to be available when required. The staff thanked the day when professional singers or actors arrived and their services were not required.

In spite of these "treats," Christmas was always a depressing time for Victoria. In 1874 she wrote to Vicky: "I have had such work choosing and ordering presents for Christmas though I began doing so in Scotland already. It increases every year beginning with 9 children—2 daughters and 4 sons-in-law and 23 grandchildren and ending with the school children at Osborne."

TABLEAU VIVANT AT OSBORNE IN JANUARY 1888
Left to right, the Hon Harriet Phipps, the Hon Marie Adeane, Major Arthur Bigge, Princess
Beatrice, Princess Henry of Battenberg as Queen Elizabeth, the Hon Alexander Yorke, Prince
Henry of Battenberg

7 The Battenbergs

*If the Queen of England thinks a person good enough for her daughter
what have other people got to say?*

Queen Victoria's mourning preoccupied her for almost 25 years from the death
of the Prince Consort. Shortly before this long period ended there was
introduced to the Queen a new family, who became of greater importance to
the Isle of Wight and to the nation as a whole than she could have imagined in
her wildest dreams. In April 1884, Princess Alice's daughter, Victoria of Hesse,
married Prince Louis of Battenberg.

At that time the Battenbergs were the morganatic family of a Royal Highness.
Although they owned a big castle in the Grand Duchy of Hesse, which Prince
Louis of Battenberg, the ultimate inheritor, sold in 1920, they were not very
wealthy, and their rank was only that of a Serene Highness. In fact, their name
was omitted from the Royal Family section of the *Almanach de Gotha* and put
in the nobility section. This, however, was eventually put right when Prince
Henry of Battenberg was created a Royal Highness by Queen Victoria. There
was considerable objection to the introduction of the family to the royal circle,
and by none more so than by Prince Wilhelm. His grandmother immediately
and sharply retaliated, saying that "Willie" deserved a good skelping for daring
to say that the Battenbergs were not *geblüt* (pure-blooded).

There were four Battenberg princes—Louis, Alexander, Henry and Francis-
Joseph. It was at Osborne that they first entered Victoria's family circle. Louis
was then thirty, clever, jolly and with a gift of impersonation that could be
wickedly funny at the expense of its victim. In December 1884 Prince Henry
came to spend Christmas at Kent House, Osborne, with Louis and his
sister-in-law Victoria, who was expecting a child. On 23 December the
Battenbergs were asked to dinner with the Queen, and it was on this occasion
that the Queen, "in dear Albert's room" faced the fact that her baby Benjamina
[Beatrice] had fallen in love with Henry. The love affair had been going on
secretly since Alice's wedding at Darmstadt eight months earlier. A most
cheerful dinner party followed the Queen's blessing on the dear child and
future son-in-law. A telegram containing the news was also sent to Beatrice's
eldest sister, Princess Victoria (not to be confused with Princess Victoria of
Hesse, referred to in the first paragraph of this chapter, who was, of course, her
niece).

The Queen, although she feared that Beatrice's marriage would mean the
loss of her last companion, was happy because her two favourite children,
Arthur and Beatrice, were at Osborne. The Queen wrote in her diary:

42

QUEEN VICTORIA AND PRINCESS BEATRICE AT OSBORNE

Reprinted from "The Life of the Queen" in the 1880 summer number of the *Graphic*. Reproduced by permission of the *Illustrated London News* Picture Library

How many prayers and thanks went up to our heavenly Father for my darling child whose birth was such a joy to us and is my blessing and comfort whom God will I know keep near me and preserved. I could but feel my heart fall in thinking the little baby Princess Beatrice, my darling one loved so much to whom he almost gave his last smile, had grown up to girlhood and to be of age and he should never have been there to guide and protect her.

Great excitement was aroused in the whole Isle of Wight when it was learnt that the wedding was to take place at Osborne. This was not the first time that one of the royal children was to marry below what was regarded as appropriate rank, for Louise had married Lord Lorne. This wedding, however, promised to be the brightest event at Osborne since the Queen went into mourning.

Henry, to please the Queen, resigned his commission in the Prussian army. He also agreed to make his permanent home with the Queen and Beatrice, so that life at Osborne could go on and flourish as before. At a special ceremony, witnessed by Princess Beatrice and the Duke of Connaught, the Queen invested Prince Henry with the Garter and conferred upon him the title of Royal Highness.

The wedding day (23 July 1885) started with a band playing below the princess's bedroom. The wedding itself gave Sir Henry Ponsonby problems, but they were solved without many hitches. The problems chiefly arose from the lack of accommodation that still existed at Osborne. A considerable number of guests who came from abroad had of necessity to stay on the island, and suitable houses nearby were soon filled up. Relatives came from the Continent after a stormy sixteen-hour crossing in the royal yacht *Victoria and Albert*. The Hessians and their suite arrived all green and yellow from seasickness. They were lodged at Osborne Cottage, Kent House, Norris Castle, Park Villa, and Cowes Castle. To cope with the overflow the royal yacht was called in to serve as a floating hotel. Other guests had to make their own arrangements, or return to the mainland after the ceremony.

For the chosen guests the question of dress was a problem, especially for the ladies, as it was unusual to hold a royal wedding in a parish church. Ladies staying in the Isle of Wight were to wear long dresses with *demi-toilette* bodies, cut down on the back, and with sleeves to the elbow. Jewels to be worn on the dress and in the hair as for full dress evening party. The Queen had laid down that only those ladies who travelled to Osborne for the day were to wear bonnets and smart morning dresses. The Duchess of Buccleuch, Mistress of the Robes, who had elicited this from the Queen, added:

> In case it may be any help to you, I will desire my dressmaker, Miss Metcalf, 111 New Bond Street, to make my "body" at once, so that anyone who cares to see it can do so by calling there.

GROUP AT THE WEDDING OF PRINCESS BEATRICE ON 23 JULY 1885 AT OSBORNE

Left to right, back row, Alexander, Prince of Bulgaria, Princess Louise of Wales, Princess Irene of Hesse, Princess Victoria of Wales, Prince Francis Joseph of Battenberg; *middle row*, Princess Maud of Wales, Princess Alix of Hesse, Princess Marie Louise and Princess Helena Victoria of Schleswig-Holstein; *front row*, Princesses Victoria Melita, Marie and Alexandra of Edinburgh, the bride and groom

45

Princess Beatrice was of stately build, with the large bosom common to all Victoria's daughters. Her wedding dress, of heavy white satin trimmed with orange blossom over a Honiton lace skirt, was looped with white heather and bouquets of entwined orange blossom. Her veil had been worn by the Queen at her own wedding.

She was given away by her mother who, after the ceremony, tenderly embraced her darling baby. "A happier-looking couple could seldom be seen kneeling at the altar together. It was very touching." The bridesmaids, "6 of whom quite children with flowing fair hair"—as the Queen wrote to Lord Tennyson—"the brilliant sunshine and the blue sea all made up pictures not to be forgotten." The Queen wore black even on this festive occasion, but of a very special material described as a grenadine-mixture double broché and double wire silk, woven on a special loom at Lyons, the set-up of which was afterwards destroyed so that the pattern could never be copied.

The Lord Chamberlain's Department and Canon Prothero of Whippingham set about the task of improvisation and decoration of the church which the Consort had rebuilt. A canvas awning covered the path from the gate to the entrance of the church, and a wooden floor was laid from the porch to the chancel. There were evergreens lightened by lilies, roses, and hot-house plants brought from Osborne House. The service was taken by the Archbishop of Canterbury, assisted by the Bishop of Winchester.

The young couple went off on a two-day honeymoon at Quarr, near Ryde, the bride wearing a dress and mantle trimmed with lace and ivory ribbon, and a small bonnet trimmed with white ostrich feathers and tied under the chin with velvet strings. She carried a little lace parasol.

To prevent a recurrence of wrangles over precedence which had marred similar occasions in the past, the order of signing the royal register was drawn up and signed by the Queen beforehand.

From the invitation list there was one very obvious omission: Mr Gladstone, the Grand Old Man who had been taken to see Princess Beatrice as a baby in the nursery. Tennyson was invited but by then he was suffering from failing sight and he wrote that he was unable to undertake the journey.

Prince Henry's yacht was illuminated and gave a display of fireworks. The festivities continued far into the night, the Queen giving a dinner and dance for the tenants and servants on the estate.

A week after the wedding Prince Henry went to the House of Lords to take the oath of allegiance.

Henry and Beatrice spent August that year at Osborne, and the Prince, who showed a great love for the sea, drove with the Queen and his wife to watch the procession of sail during the annual regatta from the Royal Yacht Squadron.

Liko (as Prince Henry was known by his family—this being an abbreviation of his own childish pronunciation "Henliko" of his nurse's Italian name for him,

"Henrico") soon got tired of following his mother-in-law and his wife about. He wanted to prove himself useful in some way, unlike Prince Christian. Liko was an excellent shot, but there was limited scope for such activities and other opportunities for employment were lacking at Osborne. The Queen's solution was to create Prince Henry Governor of the Isle of Wight. (He was already Captain-General of the Castle.) News of the appointment was welcomed, and as the Prince entered Newport the bells of St Thomas' gave "a merry peal."

The presence of Prince Henry at Osborne had not been without influence. He managed to persuade the Queen to allow smoking in a bigger and more convenient room than the bare cubby-hole previously allocated.

In due course, children arrived, to follow Gan-gan around. They were somewhat wild, and were known as "the Battenberg kids."

From 1799–1826, before Victoria's reign began, there had been a local militia in the island, the Newport Loyal Volunteers, established at Parkhurst. After the Napoleonic Wars they were disbanded; their colours hang in St Thomas' Church, Newport.

In 1859 it was decided that a new volunteer force should be raised for the defence of the island. In 1885 it acquired the title of The 5th (Isle of Wight, Princess Beatrice's) Volunteer Battalion of the Hampshire Regiment, Prince Henry being then appointed its first Honorary Colonel. He entered into his duties with great energy and took part in several field days. He endeared himself to the men, and bequeathed his dress sword to the regiment, with the request that it should be worn by the colonel at the annual inspection.

Prince Henry remained Honorary Colonel until he died in the Ashanti campaign of 1895–96. That he volunteered for that campaign is probably explained by the fact that his rather routine duties soon bored him, and Africa suggested to him some risk and adventure. Leaving his young wife and small children he set off; and then came the day, 22 January 1896, when the Queen was forced to write in her diary that Prince Arthur had come to her while she was dressing with the awful news that Liko had died of fever. The journey which brought his body home took some time. At Prince Henry's request he was to be buried in Whippingham Church. On 3 February the Queen, with the Battenberg children, went to Trinity Pier to meet the coffin. The Prince was buried with full military honours, the seamen of the *Alberta* taking charge.

The service was conducted by the Bishop of Winchester. Over the grave was built a fine memorial chapel, in which lie the remains of Princess Beatrice and her children. Every year the Queen held a memorial service there, which Marie Mallet (see Chapter 9) described as:

> [a] gloomy little funereal service. . . . These reiterated memorial services are very trying but I really think the Queen enjoys them, at any rate they are the only lode-stones that draw her within the precincts of a church!

47

8   Empress of India

*I am Empress and in common conversation am sometimes called
Empress of India*

Disraeli made his first visit to Osborne in August 1874. When stooping to kiss
Victoria's plump little hand he thought of the title by which she would be
known to him: the "Faery,"—not "Eliza" as she was irreverently called behind
her back by Ponsonby and others. Disraeli told his friend Lady Bradford: "She
was so wreathed with smiles and, as she tattled, glided about the room like a
bird."

She asked him to sit down, a privilege not accorded to a Prime Minister since
Melbourne, years ago, sat beside her, a very young Queen, on a sofa. Both the
Queen and Disraeli had lost a spouse by death, and under the grey weeping
willow of bereavement they drew together. Disraeli called snowdrops from
Osborne a Faery gift from Queen Titania herself; primroses were a sign that
"your Majesty's sceptre has touched the enchanted isle." Victoria could accept
John Brown's "wumman" with all due meekness, but to be the Faery Queen at
Osborne outdid Tennyson's "Dear and Honoured Lady." At Osborne, as
elsewhere in the Isle of Wight, the primrose grows abundantly, and one can
visualise when the flowers were in bloom the stout little figure in black moving
slowly along, with her widow attendants, picking "his favourite flower" for his
birthday, 19 April. In spite of secret discouragement from Ponsonby, the Queen
ordered everyone at Osborne to wear a primrose on the birthday of the man
who had the temerity to show imperialistic ardour.

In 1877, thanks to Disraeli, now Lord Beaconsfield, Victoria was able to send
to her beloved Prime Minister a New Year card from Osborne signed "V.R. & I."
She was now mother, grandmother, Queen and Empress. The new royal title
had its immediate effect on Osborne, and was responsible for the building of
the last wing on the great house. The design was prepared by John Lockwood
Kipling, father of Rudyard Kipling, who had been keeper of the museum at
Lahore. The intricate plasterwork was designed by Bhai Ram Singh. The design
delighted the Queen, though Kipling found fault with the pictures, which he
said had been executed by the artist "in a high state of fever." Either the fever
did not abate or tastes have changed—the pictures are no longer there.

The new wing, in spite of its failure to charm, did allow two things for which
many had occasion to be grateful. Receptions could now be held on a big scale
indoors, not in a marquee, and there was better accommodation in the rooms
above.

The adoption of India as part of her Empire could not have been more enthusiastically accepted by the Queen. Before the Durbar Room was completed, people in Cowes were already seeing the dark-skinned brightly clad Indians talking to each other in their strange language, while from the windows of upstairs rooms the shy faces of their women looked out. Indeed, the Indians (or Injuns as they were called locally) vied with the Queen's Highlanders for public attention. Portraits of most of Victoria's Indian staff line the corridor leading from the Durbar Room to the main building.

The duties of these servants varied, but undoubtedly the most important was the Munshi (an Indian word for civil servant), whose name was Hafez Abdul Karim. In the Indian corridor at Osborne there is a fine portrait of him by Swoboda.

The death of John Brown in 1883 paved the way for the Munshi's sudden advancement into a friendship with the Queen. There followed similar quarrels and disputes to those which had existed with John Brown, and Ponsonby had the old problem of making peace between the Queen's children and members of her staff. The Queen was deaf to most complaints. She studied Hindustani from the Munshi, and wanted the ladies of the court to do the same. Hindustani was not the only study: when not engaged in her lessons, the Queen discussed religion and Hindu life with the Munshi.

At Osborne the Munshi stood behind Victoria's chair to blot her signature; he cut open some of the envelopes of her correspondence; and when required he translated some of her letters into Hindustani. In later years, and especially after the death of Sir Henry Ponsonby, the Munshi became a source of acute controversy in the Queen's household. The Queen regarded any criticism of the Munshi or his cronies as insufferable interference, and fought on his behalf with all the power at her command. In the end she secured for him a CIE (Companion of the Indian Empire), which did not please the Indian Princes who had come to the Diamond Jubilee. Although fortunately the Munshi's official home was at Windsor, he had a small cottage at Osborne during the Queen's lifetime. Every Christmas he copied the Queen and gave a party for the children on the estate. His wife was not allowed to attend the party and was seen gazing wistfully at the children. It was said that if the doctor visited the Munshi's wife or aunt, a different tongue was poked out each time. After the death of the Queen, Edward VII ordered the Munshi at Osborne, as he did in all the royal houses, to destroy publicly any correspondence from the Queen.

One legend or mystery has arisen out of the building of the Durbar Room: did its construction give rise to the story that there were elephants at Osborne for which the large concrete tanks were constructed near what are now the seventh and eighth greens on the golf course? A possible explanation is that the tanks were constructed for the benefit of an elephant which was presented to the Queen, with an ape, by the Emperor of Abyssinia, and that some use was made of this elephant to carry timber during the erection of the Durbar Room.

What happened to the animals eventually is not clear: it is believed that they were presented to a zoo.

Gladstone, Disraeli's great rival, also visited Osborne many times. He had been much liked by the Prince Consort, but after the Consort's death and the emergence of the much more romantic person of Disraeli into power, Victoria found Gladstone tiresome and boring. He might please Ponsonby and his Liberal supporters, but to attack suggestions from the Grand Old Man (the GOM) as she ironically called him, braced her up as much as Disraeli's flattery. At times her talk with Gladstone could be quite friendly, if the conversation turned to such topics as the weather, old friends, or who last wore pigtails. In Gladstone's ministry of 1880–85 there took place at Osborne a constitutional struggle which recalls those with Palmerston at Windsor in the Prince Consort's time. Lord Hartington, Minister for War, failed to show the Queen a copy of her speech for the opening of Parliament in 1881. She commanded that the draft should be brought to her immediately for her to read.

Sir William Harcourt, the Home Secretary, and three other ministers arrived at Trinity Pier, East Cowes, hot and exhausted. They hurriedly drove up to Osborne in the only available vehicle, a bathing carriage, and presented themselves in the Council Chamber. Sir William, described by the Queen as more like an elephant than anything else, began somewhat boldly: "The speech of the Sovereign is only the speech of the Minister," he declared. The Queen listened in stony silence to this declaration of constitutional right, extended her hand to be kissed, and watched with malicious satisfaction as the ministers crawled and tumbled over each other to obey her gesture. Victoria felt that she had won her day "with that motley crew" before she sent them back to Westminster.

At Osborne House in 1892 the craggy old Prime Minister faced her, leaning on a stick. "You and I, Mr Gladstone, are lamer than we used to be," she cheerfully remarked. But there was none of Browning's "Grow old along with me." She subsequently noted in her diary:

> I thought him greatly altered & changed, not only much aged, walking rather bent, with a stick, but altogether; his face shrunk, deadly pale, with a weird look in his eye, a feeble expression about the mouth, and the voice altered.

Gladstone resigned from office some eighteen months later. In reply to his resignation letter she wrote: "The Queen would gladly have conferred a peerage on Mr Gladstone, but she knows that he would not accept it," as indeed he had refused to do on previous occasions.

In 1887 the Golden Jubilee burst about the Queen's ears. The festivities on the mainland nearly exhausted her, but she had to continue with further activities as soon as she neared the island. There was a review at Spithead of

QUEEN VICTORIA, WITH PRINCESS BEATRICE AND THE GRAND DUKE OF HESSE, receiving an Address from the Mayor and Corporation of Newport on 22 July 1887

20 000 officers and men, in which almost a hundred vessels took part. Although she was very tired she did not forget the Indian princes who had come over for her Jubilee, and gave them a farewell which made Ponsonby mutter objections. In spite of what she regarded as intense heat she had to drive through Cowes under banners with loyal inscriptions: "Good Sovereign—no Change required," "Fifty runs not Out," and "Better lo'ed ye canna be." Finally she collapsed in a chair at Osborne. She knew that the people in the island, in their simple and sincere way, had tried to please her, and she was pleased and contented with the result.

Three days later the Queen visited Newport. She was escorted from Osborne by members of the Isle of Wight Hunt, and the Newport Detachment of the Isle of Wight Battalion (Princess Beatrice's) furnished a guard of honour. Six bands played at different points, and an address was presented to Her Majesty by the Mayor and Corporation in St James' Square. On 26 July there was a grand children's treat in Newport, the schools being divided into the Red, the White, and the Blue. A procession was headed by the mayor, and there were a Punch-and-Judy show, see-saws and swings. On 12 August the mayor was knighted at Osborne and became Sir Francis Pittis.

Tennyson's Ode for the Golden Jubilee was not a success. His younger son, Lionel, had died of jungle fever in 1885, and the Poet Laureate's heart was not in his work. What he felt was perhaps better expressed by a draft of an ode, unpublished in his lifetime, which was found among his papers at Farringford by his son Hallam. It read:

> The noblest men methinks are bred
> Of ours the Saxo-Norman race;
> And in this world the noblest place,
> Madam, is your, our Queen and Head.
> Your name is blown on every wind,
> Your flag thro' Austral ice is borne,
> And glimmers to the northern morn,
> And floats in either Golden Ind.

As the Queen reflected on her Golden Jubilee, only one thought may have saddened her: Disraeli had died in 1881. It seemed sad that the man who had raised her to Empress should die before she celebrated her jubilee.

9 Daily Life at Osborne

Still endure

Anyone visiting Osborne in the 1880s or 1890s would have been surprised at how little anything had changed since the House was first built. The Queen's routine, when she made her regular visits at Christmas and in August, seldom varied. She still wrote in the room she had once shared with the Consort, in a voluminous black dress from which the crinoline had been removed. On her head she wore a black bonnet which resembled a miniature helmet. Her grandchildren and great-grandchildren were still expected to kiss her hand, although once four-year-old Princess Alice of Battenberg refused to do so, and being slapped by the Queen indignantly slapped her back, saying tartly "Naughty grandma!" and had to be hurried from the room.

For an intimate picture of life at Court in this period we are indebted to the letters of Marie Mallet, née Adeane, who was a Maid of Honour to the Queen from 1887 until her marriage in 1891, and Extra Woman of the Bedchamber from 1895 until the Queen's death. She came of a family that was accustomed to serve in the Household. Her mother had been for a short time a Woman of the Bedchamber. Her grandfather, Lord Hardwicke, had been a Lord in Waiting; her grandmother's brother had been for many years one of Victoria's Equerries; and an uncle, Alick Yorke, was Equerry to Prince Leopold until the latter's death, and afterwards Groom in Waiting to Her Majesty.

Before her appointment Miss Adeane was subjected to a short examination. Could she speak, read and write French and German? Could she play the piano and read easily at sight in order to play duets with Princess Beatrice? Could she ride? Was she engaged or likely to be engaged to be married? The first three questions she answered in the affirmative; the fourth in the negative. The offer of the appointment came to her while she was on holiday with her brother in Italy, and she commenced her first period of waiting at the end of December 1887. Much of the following description comes from her letters, which have been edited by her son Victor Mallet, himself a godson of Queen Victoria. The book also includes some excerpts from the diary of Marie's husband, Bernard Mallet, on his visits to the Court.

It must be remembered that by then Osborne House had a considerable staff, which was augmented by a further hundred or so when the Queen was in residence.

Summer or winter the general regularity of meals and their times continued. Breakfast was at 9.30, lunch at 2, tea at 5.30. Those attending the Queen were expected to assemble for dinner at 8.30, the Queen's own dinner being timed

53

for 8.45; but it was often 9.15 before she arrived and the company sat down, according to Miss Adeane, to a "simple meal of soup, fish, cold sirloin of beef, sweet, and dessert. The Queen's favourite fruits were oranges, pears, and monster indigestible apples, which would have daunted most people half her age, but she enjoyed them, sometimes sharing a mammoth specimen with Princess Beatrice, but more often coping with it alone. Oranges were treated in a very convenient manner, a hole cut in the top and the juice scooped out with a spoon. The Queen's dinner was timed to last exactly half an hour." The service was so fast that a slow eater, such as Marie Adeane or Gladstone, never had time to finish a most moderate helping. "Pecking like a bird," wrote Miss Adeane, "I usually managed to satisfy my hunger but could not enjoy the excellent fare handed out so expeditiously. Campbell, the Queen's Piper in kilt, etc, dispensed the Claret or Sherry, Champagne was poured out by the butlers, while the Indian servants handed the Sweets in a cat-like manner, never forgetting which particular kind of chocolate or biscuit each guest preferred, so twisting the dish in order that it could be taken with apparent ease."

When the weather was in any way suitable, the Queen breakfasted in the garden under a green-fringed parasol, surrounded by her Indian servants and a black-clad lady-in-waiting. In the afternoon the stalwart old lady, wet or shine, was driven in her carriage at a walking pace through the grounds, with Princess Mary often walking beside her. On state occasions, when there was a dinner in the Durbar Room, jewels gleamed in the hair and on the bodices of Princesses and Duchesses, in the light of electric bulbs concealed in dark blue vases. After dinner the Queen sat at a small round table and beckoned to her side those to whom she wished to speak.

"When the Queen came to Osborne," I have been told, "there was great excitement. People lined the road from Trinity Wharf to the royal entrance, to curtsy to the Queen as she went by in an open carriage. If the weather was fine, the carriage was drawn by four white horses with outriders." It was in such state that Princess Mary arrived when, in August 1893, she made her first official visit. But only Princes and Princesses like George and Mary had a real glimpse of regal life within the Osborne walls. For once arrived there the Queen seldom went outside the grounds. Fear of intrusion was no doubt largely responsible for her lack of contact with the island people after her long period of seclusion. Now and again, however, her aloofness broke down, as for example when she admired the gardens of a Mr McNann on the way to Newport, on hearing which Mr McNann sent her daily a basket of his choicest blooms. Mr Lowners Wilson records an occasion when the Queen saw a girl riding a tricycle in Newport and asked her to give a demonstration.

The Queen was not completely incurious as to what went on in the small world that surrounded her island home. One day she listened to the band at East Cowes and, impressed by the tune, sent a footman to inquire its name. I do

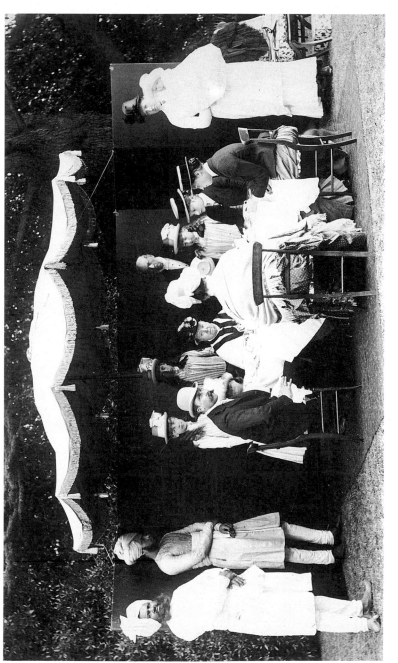

QUEEN VICTORIA BREAKFASTING IN THE GROUNDS UNDER A GREEN-FRINGED PARASOL IN AUGUST 1887
Left to right, Mohammed Baksh, Abdul Karim, Princess Marie of Edinburgh, Arthur, Duke of Connaught, Princesses
Beatrice (little girl) and Victoria Melita of Edinburgh, Queen Victoria, Princess Beatrice, Princess Henry of Battenberg
(back view), Stephen Maslin (manservant), Princess Alexandra of Edinburgh, Princesses Alex and Irene of Hesse,
nurse with Prince Alexander of Battenberg

not know what was her reply when she was told it was "Come where the beer is cheapest." Sometimes when out driving she would pass, at Carisbrooke, the convent of enclosed nuns, who she thought lived a useless, dreary existence. She took considerable interest in the Hospital at Ryde, and enjoyed visiting the Children's Ward which she opened in 1899. Marie Mallet records: "It was delightful to see her talking to the children and giving them toys."

Not all contact with the outside world could be equally agreeable. In 1887 the Queen was annoyed by the emission of smoke from the Medina Cement Works, and instructed Dr Groves, the medical officer of health, to have it stopped. He refused to act, pointing out that the smoke was yellow, not black, and therefore permissible by the terms of the Smoke Abatement Act which she had signed. The Queen accepted this reply, and apologised for wasting Dr Groves' time.

Relations were of course closer with the tenants on the Osborne estate. Sentimental stories are told of her reading the Bible to old tenants, and she was said to have entered some houses unannounced and even to have tasted the potatoes cooking for dinner, declaring them to be better than those at the House. On the whole such visits, though kindly meant, were not appreciated, and some tenants took care not to be at home when she called. Others found the Queen "wonderfully kind." There were a doctor and a trained nurse at Osborne whose services were available to the tenants. When the daughter of the bailiff on the estate died the family quickly received a personal note from the Queen, who also sent them a fine memorial brooch mounted with the dead girl's hair.

Appropriate recognition of the Queen's attention was expected in return. Miss Thompson, daughter of one of the tenants, told me: "The Queen used to come to New Barn to visit my mother, and sometimes asked to see the children. The footman used to open the door and call out: 'The Queen's here,' and we children used to file out and go to the side of her carriage and shake hands with the Queen."

"Harvest home" was the occasion of an annual gathering of the tenants. The grown-ups had a meat tea, and the children had sports and a simpler meal. Seated in her carriage the Queen distributed the prizes.

She was rarely allowed to know much about the sufferings of her subjects generally, but when she was informed she showed a very sincere distress. On 20 August 1845, accompanied by her husband, Victoria visited Parkhurst Prison. It was then a jail for young criminals, and was reputed to house the refuse of the underworld. The young prisoners spent the first two months in solitary confinement, which Victoria found "triste and lonely." She asked for a free pardon for the most deserving in each ward.

On 15 January 1864 Queen Victoria paid another visit. She had been reading some pamphlets on prison reform and had consulted with Elizabeth Fry on the subject. This time most of the children had been removed. The women prisoners were largely prostitutes awaiting transportation to Australia, and their children, who would be sent to an orphanage. The Queen was greeted with curses mingled with cries for mercy, and though she was attended by the Prison Governor and the senior wardress she was horrified and beat a hasty retreat, never to visit the prison again.

Marie Adeane's period of waiting on the Queen included several Christmases at Osborne, and from her descriptions of them, and from notes in her husband's diary, it is possible to piece together a picture of what went on. It is clear that for the royal household Christmas was a most active and demanding time. Then, as nowadays, those journeying to the island faced hazards from fog or stormy weather. "We have been enveloped in dense fog for four days," wrote Marie Adeane in January 1888, "and got no letters yesterday, as the steamers won't run in such dangerous weather. We have had to go out just as usual but it is odious and even the Queen complains of the damp." In such a fog Bernard Mallet travelled to Osborne in 1897 to attend at the household tree, at which the Queen distributed her household gifts—and most handsome presents they were. Marie herself received "a case of large silver gilt spoons, the usual pocket-book, and some odds and ends, including a man of gingerbread, a German custom."

Services on Christmas Day do not appear to have been inspiring. During her first stay at Osborne Marie reported: "We had an apology for a service at 11.0—no lessons, psalms or prayers, only litany and hymns and sermon from Canon Duckworth." She emphasised the Queen's objecting to taking communion more than two or three times a year. Nevertheless when, in 1900, she saw the Queen at that service for the first time, "[i]t was a touching little ceremony, the Queen . . . leaning on her stick and supported by Princess Thora [Victoria of Schleswig-Holstein], she cannot kneel on account of her lame leg. . . ."

On another occasion Bernard Mallet noted in his diary that after tea on Christmas Eve the household was summoned to the Durbar Room to see the royal presents, after which "The whole household, including myself, dined with the Queen . . . Baron of beef, woodcock pie . . . boar's head displayed on sideboard."

Boxing Day was a great day for Christmas cards all round. The children on the estate were not forgotten, and were expected to attend a special tea, the boys dressed in sailor suits. When the Queen entered at 5.30 families were expected to line up in age order. The presents were dolls, tea or dinner services, and books for the boys.

A charming little story was told by Michael Smith, son of Canon Clement Smith, Vicar of Whippingham. Michael was a choirboy at the time, and the youngest of a large family, of whom the rest were all girls. On this occasion he

CHRISTMAS TREES AND PRESENTS IN THE DURBAR ROOM, 1900

was told by his mother to be home immediately after the tea. As he had to walk to Whippingham, he left in good time. His going, however, was noticed by one of the Court ladies in charge, and he was told that he ought to wait for the Queen's arrival; but Michael insisted on obeying his mother. Imagine the surprise of the family when the next day the Queen, preceded by her Indian servants, arrived to bring a special book for Michael, and to give it to him herself for being such a good boy in obeying his mother. For several years after that the Queen sent the lad a special book at Christmas, signed personally by her.

Summer at Osborne also had disadvantages for those who attended the Queen in July and August. There was golf and tennis, but neither was very attractive and there were limits to amusement. In 1888 Marie Adeane wrote: "I have been playing lawn tennis with Princess Alex [Princess of Wales] and her Lady in Waiting; they can neither of them get a ball over the net so the game was not exhilarating." Ten years later she had hoped to see the yacht races, but "[o]ur sitting room at tea-time reminds me of 'The Black Hole of Calcutta,' the butter melts, Lady Erroll pours out the tea as strong as brandy and we all perspire and wish we were in our humble homes. . . . I am reading 'Hilda Stafford' to the Queen in the small hours of the morning, a story by the author of 'Ships that pass in the night' and equally gloomy and consumptive."

One of the more tiresome of Marie's occupations resulted from the revival of the "treats," or amateur entertainments, which the Queen had enjoyed so much years ago. "It is extraordinary," wrote Eddy [Albert, Duke of Clarence] to his brother George [later King George V] "how pleased Grandmama is with such small things." He had on this occasion, February 1891, been specially summoned to attend one of these treats.

The Court News reported these entertainments, with tableaux such as "The Queen of Sheba," "Carmen," "Queen Elizabeth and Raleigh." All rehearsals were carefully supervised by the Queen, and such plays as *The Rivals* were edited by her as she thought best.

On Tuesdays there were concerts at which famous artists were invited to appear. On some occasions fine singers and orchestras came, but the Queen did not always approve. Once Madame Nordica was engaged, much to the Queen's disgust, as she admired neither her voice nor her person. "I will *not*," she said emphatically, "hear Nordica."

Dull as life might usually be for the young people on the staff at Osborne, there were moments when they could stoke up the fires in the cold rooms after the Queen had gone to bed. Marie Adeane recounted one such occasion: "I dined with the household, but at ten we all marched to the drawing room and were stared at as usual until ¼ to 11, when the Queen having been safely seen upstairs, we adjourned to the council room and danced on a carpet to the sound of a piano mecanique turned alternately by the Duchess of Albany and

Col. Carrington. It really was very comical. Prince Henry [of Battenberg] got tremendously excited and pranced about all over the place, he nearly whirled me off my legs, for he dances in the German fashion and plunges horribly. At 5 minutes to 12 we all adjourned to an ante-room where we were supposed to partake of punch of an extremely potent character . . . I procured some lemonade . . . after these potations we all became very merry and someone proposed 'consequences' . . . a quire of paper and fifteen pencils appeared as if by magic, and we sat round a huge table and were bidden to write whatever came into our heads, the results read out . . . were perfectly killing; needless to say we all came in for our share, the junior Maid of Honour not escaping, and hiding her blushes behind a certain grey feather fan. . . . At last, about 1 o'clock breathless with laughter we retired to rest, having quite enjoyed ourselves, a somewhat rare event in these regions."

As the Queen grew older she attended the royal pew in Whippingham church less frequently and relied more on her own chapel at Osborne House. Low church though she was, she gave the chapel a fine silver cross, which was later placed at the head of her coffin when she lay in state. The music for the chapel was supplied by an American organ which was wheeled about as required, and in consequence never was in the best playing condition. Bernard Mallet, who describes the chapel as "a long low ugly room" states that the building and decoration of it cost between £5000 and £6000.

As the Queen expressed strong views on church matters, and was nearer being a Presbyterian than an Anglican, she was careful to appoint as the Bishop of Winchester (in which diocese the Isle of Wight then was) and also the Dean of Windsor, men after her own heart. This selectivity extended also to the choice of preachers for Osborne. In 1879 the Dean of Windsor proposed seven names, but the Queen objected to nearly all of them. Her comments were as follows:

NAME	QUEEN'S REMARKS
The Dean of Westminster	*Too long*
The Dean of Christchurch	Sermons are like lectures
Dr. Bradley	Excellent man but tiresome preacher
Mr. Roberts	X
Mr. Birch	X
Mr. Tarver	X
Mr. Rowsell	

The Queen likes none of these for the House. The last of all is the *only good* Preacher excepting Dean Stanley & he is too long. Mr. Rowsell unfortunately reads very disagreeably but those crossed are most disagreeable Preachers and the Queen *wonders* the Dean cd mention them. . . .

BARTON MANOR IN 1867

Three years later the Queen was quick to show that she was governor of the Church of England when the death of Gerald Wellesley made it necessary to appoint a new Dean of Windsor. In a letter to Sir Henry Ponsonby the Queen wrote:

> The Queen is glad that Mr. Gladstone sees that the appointment of Dean of Windsor is a personal & not a political appointment; she will therefore *not* expect Mr. Gladstone to suggest names to her.

Modernisation of Osborne House went on very slowly. A lift was introduced, enabling Victoria to reach the first floor, but it was a hand-worked affair, so that only she could profit by it. In August 1898 Marie Mallet wrote: "The Queen speaks into a phonograph this afternoon in order to send a verbal message to King Menelik."

When the Queen heard of Marconi's invention of wireless she determined to see the apparatus for herself, and the opportunity came when the Prince of Wales injured his knee in Paris and retired to convalesce in the royal yacht *Osborne*, moored off Cowes for the regatta in 1898. The Prince was doubtless unwilling to submit to his aged mother's concern for his health, so he had the royal yacht moored out of sight of the house. The Queen invited Marconi to rig up his apparatus at Ladywood Cottage, in the grounds of Osborne, and to maintain regular communication with the yacht. During that August about 150 messages were received from the Prince and his doctor, some quite lengthy; these were passed on to the Queen.

David Gunston, in his book *Marconi—Father of Radio* records that on one occasion when Marconi was fixing up his equipment he saw the Queen walk by, and greeted her, doffing his hat. She was annoyed at what she considered an unjustified liberty from a stranger, completely ignored him, and sent a message by a gardener that Marconi should "go back and round," so as to avoid crossing the Queen's path. Marconi was so offended at this that he threatened to leave at once, but on being told this the Queen merely gave instructions to "get another electrician." However, after it had been explained to her that the Italian was no ordinary electrician all ended happily; she gave Marconi an audience and wished him success in his work.

Meanwhile Barton Manor continued to be used to house members of the staff and of the Queen's family. It was described by Alick Yorke as "a farmhouse where the Equerries and Grooms reside in lonely grandeur and live in mortal fear of rats and ghosts besides having to go some distance to their meals." Sir Frederick Ponsonby, coming to it in the 1890s, described it as "quite comfortable, but it necessitated a brougham being ordered to take [the equerries] to dinner and bring them back to bed. . . . The house was filled with paintings, which were really first-rate. . . ."

10   Yachts and Yacht Clubs

*I assure you I wish I cld avoid ever going on the sea again wh, as we happen
to be an Island & Osborne is one, is impossible*

Queen Victoria could not spend so many years at Osborne without developing
considerable interest in yachts and yachting. Her first visits to the Isle of Wight
were made on the yacht *Emerald*, a cutter of 118 tons, and quite early in her
reign she arranged for the building for herself of the first of a series of steam
yachts, each of which was named *Victoria and Albert*. The earliest, of 1049
tons, was launched in April 1843; it was commanded by Lord Adolphus
Fitzclarence, and manned by the officers and crew of the *Royal George*, who
were transferred to her. In August of the same year she took the Queen and
Prince Albert on their state visit to King Louis Philippe of France at the Château
d'Eu. The Queen, however, soon complained that she was too slow, and
twelve years later the second *Victoria and Albert*, a paddle-steamer of 2000
tons, replaced her. This remained in service for many years, although the
Queen also found fault with her, as being too small compared with the yachts of
the Czar and the Kaiser:

> The royal yacht *Victoria and Albert* (she wrote to Lord Salisbury) is no
> longer in accord with our dignity as the head of a great maritime state and
> is the subject of continuous comment among our relations on the
> Continent.

Eventually, this *Victoria and Albert* was in her turn replaced by the third of that
name, launched in 1899, but because of a mishap at her launching was not
ready for service until 1900. Even then she was much criticised. Marie Mallet
wrote:

> . . . she *must* be but a makeshift. It is really disgraceful that the Sovereign
> of the first Maritime Power in the world could have no better vessel in
> which to put to sea. . . .

In addition to these yachts, the Queen had a smaller vessel, the *Fairy*, a screw
steamer of 260 tons, which acted as a tender. For example, when in July 1845
the King of Holland visited Osborne, it was in the newly built *Fairy* that Prince
Albert met him at Portsmouth and brought him to Cowes. But when, later in the
day, the royal party went for a cruise, it was on board the *Victoria and Albert*.
Again when, in the following month, the Queen attended her first Regatta, it
was in the *Fairy* that she followed the racing yachts.

Later in the reign other ships had to be pressed into service in emergencies.

A change of Ministry in 1886 involved much coming and going, and Sir Henry Ponsonby described the resulting activity in a letter to Horace Seymour, one of the Private Secretaries in Downing Street:

> The Solent is covered with steamers carrying Ministers hither and luncheons are prepared in various rooms for such as must go at 2, at 2.30 and at 3. The Queen's yacht *Elfin* has gone to look for some of them at Portsmouth. The Queen's launch *Louise* is searching about Cowes Harbour for others. The Queen's yacht *Alberta* has gone to Southampton for the Duchess of Edinburgh. So our Navy is well employed.

Another royal yacht, the *Osborne*, built about 1874, was used by the Prince of Wales and lesser royalty.

It was in the *Fairy* that the Queen encountered the first of two accidents met with between the island and Portsmouth. In October 1848 the royal family was approaching Portsmouth when those on board the *Fairy* noticed some people in the water. The Queen wrote to her uncle Leopold about the event:

> Our voyage yesterday was much saddened by a terrible accident at Spithead, which delayed us half an hour, and which still fills us with horror. The sea was running very high, and we were just outside what is called The Spit, when we saw a man in the water, sitting on the keel of a boat, and we stopped, and at that moment Albert discerned *many heads* above the sea, including a poor woman. The tide was running so strong that we could only stop an instant and let a boat down, but you may imagine our horror. We waited at Gosport to hear if the people had been saved, and learnt that three had, two of whom by our *Fairy's* boat, and that four were drowned. Very horrid indeed.

Other bystanders on the royal yacht described how Albert threw up his arms and called out again and again to stop the yacht's engines in the hope of helping. Not merely the Queen but all the royal party were on board and saw it all. The captain refused to stop the ship's engines. "You may order it yourself, sir," he said, "but on your own responsibility." No doubt the captain was right. To stop a vessel the size of the *Fairy* and going at the rate she was, would have worsened the situation and imperilled the lives of those on board.

A second accident, some twenty-seven years later, directly involved the Queen's yacht *Alberta*. In August 1875, while steaming at 17 knots in daylight, in calm weather and good visibility, she rammed and sank the yacht *Mistletoe* sailing close-hauled from Portsmouth to Ryde. Sir Henry Ponsonby thereupon issued requests that private yachts should keep well clear of the royal yacht, but there was a strong feeling among the yachting fraternity at the time that the seamanship of the *Alberta* was poor. It is said that the Queen and Princess Beatrice were on deck at the time, and that the Princess drew the Queen's

THE PRINCE AND PRINCESS OF WALES AND THEIR CHILDREN ON HMY *OSBORNE* IN 1880
Left to right, Princess Maud, Princess Louise, Princess Victoria (on the floor), Prince Albert Victor and Prince George

attention to the proximity of the *Mistletoe* just before the collision. The Queen was certainly horrified by the accident. Three days after it she wrote to her daughter Victoria:

> . . . Nothing will ever efface from our minds the horror of the scene; I hear the crash now and feel the shock—see the poor lady in her calm, silent despair and the poor dying old man. . . . No blame can I feel sure be attached to my people on board the *Alberta*. They behaved admirably and had it not been for their promptitude I am sure that no one would have been saved.

But despite the Queen's opinion, matters could not rest there. The captain of the *Mistletoe* (the "poor old man" mentioned by the Queen), the mate, and a Miss Peel, sister-in-law of the owner (Mr E S Heywood) were all drowned. Following the inquest, the Admiralty announced on 28 December its decision that Staff Captain Welch was responsible for the collision, as his senior officer, Captain H S H Prince Ernest of Leiningen, was on duty with Her Majesty below decks. This did not, however, appease yachtsmen, and Mr Heywood received an apology and £3000 compensation. Even that did not end the matter, for on 10 April 1876, there was a rather acrimonious debate about the incident in Parliament.

When Victoria came to the throne there were two yacht clubs in the vicinity of the Solent—the Royal Yacht Squadron at Cowes, and the Royal Southern Yacht Club at Southampton. The former, to which her uncle King William IV, who was a member, had given the privilege of flying the white ensign, was regarded by many, including the Queen, as unrivalled; it was the most exclusive club in the whole country. Its position was reinforced towards the end of her reign by the Prince of Wales becoming its Commodore. However, the Queen herself never had any very intimate connection with the Squadron; there was not even a place for her on its premises, and the Prince Consort, who was never a good sailor, preferred hunting stags at Balmoral to yachting.

The Royal Southern Yacht Club flew the blue Ensign.

On 24 May 1845, the Queen's birthday, a third non-exclusive club was founded, and named in her honour the Royal Victoria Yacht Club. *Hunt's Yachting Magazine* remarked that its founding was "in commemoration of the honour conferred on the Isle of Wight by Her Most Gracious Majesty in having chosen Osborne House for a marine palace." A year later Prince Albert laid the foundation stone of the club house, on the sea front close to Ryde Pier; it is now the Prince Consort Hotel. Yachts from this club were authorised to fly the red ensign of Her Majesty's fleet, for which reason the club was for many years known as "The Red Squadron."

The first regatta of the new club was held on 4 August 1845. Just before the third race, for yachts and gigs up to 25ft (7.6m), the Queen and the Prince

Consort arrived off Ryde in the *Fairy* ". . . and were received [as the *Yachtsman's Annual and General Register* for 1845 recorded] with every demonstration of honour and loyalty from the countless thousands assembled."

In 1857 an unfortunate accident marred the Royal Victoria regatta. As the guns before the club house were being fired in honour of the departing Emperor of the French, one exploded, injuring two of the signalmen, one seriously. Inquiries revealed that the gun had previously been imperfectly cleaned, by the use of a sponge intended for one of smaller calibre. The Queen made a contribution to a subscription for the seriously injured man.

It was the Royal Yacht Squadron that was responsible for the annual Cowes Regatta and also for the British entry into the race with the schooner *America* in 1851. A happier incident is recorded in connection with this race.

The royal party, on board the second *Victoria and Albert*, were awaiting the outcome of the race in Alum Bay, and the onlookers were delighted to see a boat put off from the royal yacht with Prince Albert and the Prince of Wales, then aged nine, in the stern. They landed under the cliff in Alum Bay, and the young Prince, in white sailor's suit and tarpaulin hat, was observed dancing down the shady road with boyish vivacity. As the *America* rounded the Needles, she lowered her ensign to the royal yacht; Commodore Stevens took off his hat, and all the crew, following his example, remained with uncovered heads for some minutes until they had passed the *Victoria and Albert*, a mark of respect for the Queen.

THE ROYAL YACHT *OSBORNE* IN 1880

11 The White Queen

The old year dies—God beckons those we love

In September 1896, when Victoria had been on the throne for 59 years, 3 months, and 5 days, her reign became the longest of any British monarch's, a record previously held by her grandfather, George III. By then she could have echoed the words of Charles Lamb: "All, all are gone, the old familiar faces." Although her own health remained good on the whole, as the years passed friends and relatives left her. Not all of them were so old, either. Princess Alice, who had looked after the Queen so well when she came to Osborne for the first time in her widowhood, died in 1878, by a strange coincidence on the anniversary of her father's, the Consort's, death; and in 1884 Prince Leopold, Duke of Albany, died in the south of France.

In January 1892 the Queen's grandson Eddy, Duke of Clarence, died at Sandringham, and although he had not been a frequent visitor to Osborne his death added one more to the lozenge-shaped memorials in the royal pew in Whippingham Church. Eighteen months later his brother, George (later King George V), married Princess Mary of Teck, who had been the Duke of Clarence's fiancée, and of their marriage was born David, later Edward VIII (1894), Bertie, later George VI (1895) and Mary (1900).

The death of the Duke of Clarence called for another ode from the aged Poet Laureate. He wrote to the Queen: "I know that Your Majesty has a perfect trust in the Love and Wisdom which order the circumstances of our life and in this alone is there comfort." His ode had a similar theme.

In 1895 Sir Henry Ponsonby died at Osborne Cottage, where he and his family had lived in latter years. The Queen lost no time in visiting Lady Ponsonby with a message of condolence. She was aware that she had lost a genial and loyal servant who understood her unpredictable ways. Prince Alfred was fatally ill with an unidentified disease, from which he died in July 1900; his son predeceased him, dying of consumption in February 1899. Victoria's favourite daughter, the Dowager Empress of Germany, was also approaching her end, dying of cancer of the spine, although she briefly outlived her mother.

One of the main problems experienced by the Queen's entourage was providing her with a guard. She loathed any form of protection and any interference with her mode of travel. Gone were the days when she could rely on John Brown, who would doggedly sit on the box of her carriage and prevent any of her subjects from getting near her or even seeing her. Brown was dead and there was too much trouble about for any risks to be taken. There were Fenians from Ireland; dangers from radicals, even republicans. It was felt

68

QUEEN VICTORIA WITH SOME OF HER GREAT-GRANDCHILDREN IN
AUGUST 1900
Prince Edward (later Edward VIII) standing, Prince Albert (later George VI), Princess
Mary and the baby, Prince Henry of York

69

accordingly that when the Queen was in residence she must be guarded. The Isle of Wight authorities acquired a small barracks that had long existed near Parkhurst Prison, and for many years, even after the Queen's death, this was the official barracks for the Osborne guard unit. When the Queen was actually at Osborne the guards were sent from the Parkhurst barracks to the Victoria and Albert barracks on the East Cowes front.

The Kaiser continued to irritate the Queen, and under the influence of Bismarck sent her such letters and matrimonial advice as caused her to instruct her Ambassador in Berlin to discourage him from making his annual visits. While at Osborne in 1895 he picked a quarrel with Lord Salisbury, the Prime Minister, and annoyed both the Queen and the Prince of Wales by being late for dinner, causing the Prince to be late also, and referring to the latter audibly as "the old popinjay." At the end of that year he sent a telegram of congratulation to President Kruger on the failure of the Jameson Raid which threw the Queen into a rage. The Prince of Wales urged his mother to forbid the Kaiser to come to Cowes in 1896, and while she did not administer the "good snub" which he had suggested, she noted in her journal: "Sent off my letter to William in which I gave him a piece of my mind as to his dreadful telegram," later informing his mother that the anger which he had caused would "last for some little time." It was not until 1899 that the Kaiser's huge white yacht, *Hohenzollern*, was once more invited to the Solent.

In 1897 the Diamond Jubilee was celebrated by festivities similar to those that had taken place ten years earlier. Again the Queen visited Newport, but by now she tired very easily, and her sight was much impaired.

By 1899 the Queen's health was beginning to show signs of deterioration. Her eyesight was so much impaired that she wrote her instructions to her staff in large print, with purple or black chalk which smudged and could not be read. Yet she still refused to pass on any duties to the heir to the throne. The last two years of her life were marred by the war in South Africa, but she was undaunted by the thought of defeat and pressed on in a manner which would have challenged many younger than herself: "The Queen was as brave as a lion," wrote Marie Mallet. ". . . Still she looked so anxious and care-worn and the worry will tell upon her health. . . . We are all, from the Queen downwards, making things for the troops, caps, cholera belts, socks and waistcoats, the Queen turns out khaki comforters as if her bread depended on it, and says so sweetly 'I think I am doing something for my soldiers, although it is so little.' "

In 1900, in spite of better news from South Africa, "this horrible year" brought no relief. Storms rocked the Solent, and the bathing pontoon was smashed. In the autumn Victoria went on her annual visit to Balmoral; in spite of the infirmities of old age and what her son-in-law, Lord Lorne, called some "little wildering of a tired brain," her heart showed sufficient strength to make the annual visit seem possible. However, the threatening grey skies of the north

DIAMOND JUBILEE PROCESSION IN NEWPORT ON 24 JULY 1897

Queen Victoria with Princess Beatrice (next to her), Princess Aribert of Anhalt and Princess Victoria Eugenie of Battenberg (both back views)

drove her southward to Windsor. After a short stay her chest showed further signs of weakness, and she was brought in an exhausted condition to Osborne. There she lay in a sort of restless slumber. She sent out a few cards for the New Year, including one to Lord Salisbury on which in her shaky writing were the words "The old year dies, God beckons those he loves."

On 15 January 1901 she issued her last dispatch. Three days later a Court Circular was published saying that "the Queen should be kept perfectly quiet and should abstain for the present from transacting publick business." The principal physician who attended on the Queen during her last hours was Sir James Reid; two other physicians were also there. On the 19th a fairly optimistic bulletin was issued, to the effect that the Queen's strength had been maintained and there were indications of a slight improvement in the evening. Nevertheless the Vicar of Whippingham was summoned to Osborne.

Naturally anxiety was felt, and East Cowes must have been hard pressed to deal with the coming and going of important visitors. Mr Balfour arrived to represent the government, and the Bishop of Winchester shared with the Vicar of Whippingham the reading of prayers and hymns. The Archbishop of Canterbury was sent for, but it seems he arrived too late, if at all. On the 19th the Prince of Wales was sent for, and also the Duke of Connaught, who was in Germany at the time. On the 20th there were two bulletins, that in the evening reading "The Queen's condition has late this evening become more serious with increased weakness and diminished powers of taking nourishment." By this time all the Queen's family had been summoned to her side. *The Illustrated London News* of that date states that Victoria's grandson, the German Kaiser, in the midst of the celebration of the bicentenary of the foundation of the Prussian monarchy, countermanded all festivities and hastily travelled to England. He arrived at Osborne on the 21st, and allowing for the differences between uncle and nephew he received a cordial greeting. He was accompanied by his wife and the Crown Prince. His mother, Victoria's daughter, was too ill to come.

In the meantime reporters were collecting outside Osborne, each one anxious to be the first to report the news, and the Post Office installed extra telephones to cope with the rush. In the house the old Queen, unconscious of what was going on, opened her eyes once or twice to listen to the clergy or to seek out some familiar face. Once she rallied shortly and asked if she could have her favourite dog Turi on the bed with her. Lady Longford says this was done. Perhaps she recalled dimly the occasion when, after her coronation, she rushed upstairs to bath her dog Dash. On this later occasion the dog stayed only a few minutes.

Propped up by Dr Reid and the Kaiser, Victoria breathed more and more quietly in the gathering gloom. As the words of "Lead, kindly light" were read by the clergy her eyes appeared to open; "And in the morn those angel faces smile, Which I have loved long since and lost awhile." Each of the family knelt

QUEEN VICTORIA'S COFFIN DRAPED WITH STATE ROBES AT OSBORNE HOUSE IN JANUARY 1901

in turn by her bed and whispered his or her name. At about four o'clock she asked for the Prince of Wales. "Bertie," she whispered, and was silent for ever.

The last bulletin read: "Osborne House, January 22. Her Majesty the Queen breathed her last at 6.45 p.m., surrounded by her children and grandchildren." It was signed by James Reid, MD, Douglas Powell, MD, and Thomas Barlow, MD.

Whatever quiet may have reigned in the house, there was little chance of it outside. No sooner had Superintendent Fraser communicated the official news to the waiting reporters than there was a race for the telephones, some cycling down the hill at breakneck speed. One local man earned £1 for leading the reporters to the specially installed telephone booths at East Cowes. Even the great-grandchildren, loosed from their parents, were for a short time shouting out that Gan-gan was dead. No doubt Queen Victoria would have strongly objected to this noisy behaviour, but one must remember that here in the Isle of Wight was the end of a whole century, and the beginning of a new with a King. Perhaps she would have understood.

Victoria's body was placed by her two sons, the Prince of Wales and the Duke of Connaught, in a white coffin. The Queen had always disliked black trappings, preferring purple and white, and she had been particularly impressed by the description of Tennyson's funeral, when the coffin was draped in white and covered by a pall on which were embroidered the words from "Crossing the Bar." Her own was covered by a pall bearing the royal arms in gold and white which the School of Church Embroidery worked fast to produce.

With considerable satisfaction Lord Lorne records that no undertakers or employees outside the estate were needed for the funeral. The catafalque was placed in the dining room, where special pictures were hung, all the rest being removed or covered with black hangings. On the Queen's tiny frame had been placed her wedding veil and bunches of primroses—already in bloom, for the weather was warm for the time of year.

The day of the procession from Osborne was exceptionally calm and bright. All walked on foot to accompany the gun carriage on its way to East Cowes. The only funeral march played was Chopin's. An American lady was nearly lynched because she was standing watching unsuitably dressed, not in mourning. At the Medina the coffin was borne on to the *Alberta*, which, guarded by six destroyers, slowly sailed away to the sound of the minute guns. How Victoria had disliked this "popping"! As darkness gathered above Gosport (from where the coffin was taken to London by train), sunshine broke out again on the Osborne lawn. But the room with the balcony and bay window remained with its blinds down until Queen Elizabeth II, Queen Victoria's great-great-granddaughter, raised them and let the light in again.

QUEEN VICTORIA'S FUNERAL PROCESSION LEAVING OSBORNE HOUSE ON 1 FEBRUARY 1901

Acknowledgements

I am grateful to Mr J Keith Horsefield, CB, DSc, without whom this book would never have been completed. I must thank, too, those people from East Cowes and other parts of the island who have so kindly assisted me with reminiscences of Queen Victoria's life at Osborne and the traditions which she left behind. I am particularly grateful to Mr E Sibbick and Mr R E Brinton, who have given me valuable information about the island and Osborne House. Miss Jones, the Librarian at Osborne, has constantly given me patient help, and has researched the answers to many questions. The information for my chapter on the royal yachts was largely supplied by my friend Colonel G R Stevens, OBE, a keen yachtsman, who consulted the records of the Royal Yacht Squadron and the Royal Victoria Yacht Club. To Dr R R Prewer I owe my thanks for his assistance in identifying the Queen's social work in hospitals and prisons. Sir Robin Mackworth-Young, Librarian of Windsor Castle, has been good enough to read the manuscript and to assist me on certain points.

I am naturally indebted in large degrees to the many authors who have previously written about Queen Victoria and her times. A list of the books which I have consulted is on the next page.

I gratefully acknowledge the gracious permission of Her Majesty The Queen to republish certain material of which she owns the copyright.

I am grateful also to Mr Victor Mallet and to John Murray (Publishers) Ltd for permission to quote from *Life with Queen Victoria: Marie Mallet's Letters from Court* 1887–1901.

Lady Longford has very kindly permitted me to quote from her invaluable biography *Victoria RI*.

I appreciate also permission from Macmillan London and Basingstoke to quote from *Sir Henry Ponsonby, His Life from his Letters* by Arthur Ponsonby.

The late Sir Charles Tennyson was good enough to allow me to quote from *Dear and Honoured Lady*, edited by Hope Dyson and himself.

The bust of Queen Victoria (1841) by Chantry that is shown on the front cover is reproduced by permission of the National Portrait Gallery, London.

Arnold Florance
1977

Works Consulted

Baillie and Bolitho (eds)	Letters of Lady Augusta Stanley (1927)
ditto	Later Letters of Lady Augusta Stanley (1929)
Benson, A C and Viscount Esher (eds)	The Letters of Queen Victoria, A Selection from Her Majesty's Correspondence, First Series, 1837–61: 3 vols (1907)
Bolitho, Hector	The Reign of Queen Victoria (1949)
Buckle, G E (ed)	The Letters of Queen Victoria, A Selection from Her Majesty's Correspondence, Second Series, 1862–85, 3 vols (1926)
ditto	ditto, Third Series, 1886–1901, 3 vols (1930)
Bullock, Charles	The Queen's Resolve . . . [?1901]
	Catalogue of the Principal Items on view at Osborne House (1966)
Chancellor, Frank B	Prince Consort (1931)
Charlton, John	Osborne House (1970)
Creston, Dormer	The Youthful Queen Victoria (1952)
Cullen, Tom	The Empress Brown (1969)
de Soissons, Count	The True Story of the Empress Eugénie [1920]
Duff, David	The Shy Princess (1958)
Dyson, Hope and Tennyson, Charles (eds)	Dear and Honoured Lady (1969)
Eldridge, R J	Newport, Isle of Wight, in Bygone Days (1952)
Epton, Nina	Victoria and her Daughters (1971)
Esher, Viscount (ed)	The Girlhood of Queen Victoria, A Selection from Her Majesty's Diaries between the years 1832 and 1840, 2 vols (1912)
Fulford, Roger	Dearest Child: Letters between Queen Victoria and the Princess Royal, 1858–1861 (1964)
ditto	Darling Child: Letters between Queen Victoria and the Princess Royal, 1871–1878 (1976)
ditto	The Prince Consort (1949)
Hassell, J	Tour of the Isle of Wight, 2 vols (1790)
Helps, Arthur (ed)	Leaves from the Journal of our Life in the Highlands from 1848 to 1861 (1868)
Holmes, Sir R R	Queen Victoria, 1819–1901 (1901)
Howarth, Patrick	The Year is 1851 (1951)
Jones, Barbara	The Isle of Wight (1950)
Lee, Sir Sidney	Queen Victoria (1904)

Longford, Lady	Victoria, R.I. (1964)
Lorne, Marquess of	VRI, Her Life and Empire [?1902]
Lutyens, Mary (ed)	Lady Lytton's Court Diary (1961)
Magnus, Sir Philip	King Edward the Seventh (1964)
Mallet, Victor	Life with Queen Victoria: Marie Mallet's letters from Court 1887–1901 (1968)
Martin, Sir Theodore	Life of the Prince Consort, 5 vols (1875–80)
Nicolson, Sir Harold	King George the Fifth (1952)
Ponsonby, Arthur	Henry Ponsonby—His Life from his Letters (1942)
Ponsonby, Sir Frederick	Recollections of Three Reigns (1951)
ditto	Sidelights on Queen Victoria (1930)
Pope-Hennessy, James	Queen Mary (1959)
Quigley, DJ	The Isle of Wight Rifles (nd)
Raymond, J (ed)	Queen Victoria's Early Letters (1963)
Sara, ME	The Life and Times of HRH Princess Beatrice (1945)
Stanley, Hon Eleanor	Twenty Years at Court (1916)
Stachey, Lytton	Queen Victoria (1948)
Tisdall, EEP	Queen Victoria's Private Life (1961)
Trevelyan, GM	Illustrated English Social History, vol 4: The Nineteenth Century (1957)
Turner, WJ (ed)	Impressions of English Literature (1947)
Watson, Vera	A Queen at Home (1952)
Wyndham, Mrs H (ed)	Correspondence of Sarah Spencer, Lady Lyttleton (1912)
	The Gentlewoman (various dates)
	The Illustrated London News (various dates)
	The Isle of Wight County Press (various dates)

WHIPPINGHAM CHURCH

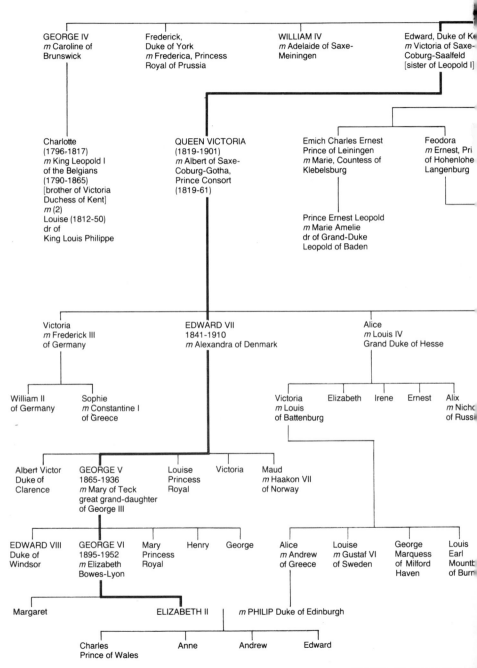

KING GEOR
(1738-1820)

GEORGE IV
m Caroline of
Brunswick

Frederick,
Duke of York
m Frederica, Princess
Royal of Prussia

WILLIAM IV
m Adelaide of Saxe-
Meiningen

Edward, Duke of Ke
m Victoria of Saxe-
Coburg-Saalfeld
[sister of Leopold I]

Charlotte
(1796-1817)
m King Leopold I
of the Belgians
(1790-1865)
[brother of Victoria
Duchess of Kent]
m (2)
Louise (1812-50)
dr of
King Louis Philippe

QUEEN VICTORIA
(1819-1901)
m Albert of Saxe-
Coburg-Gotha,
Prince Consort
(1819-61)

Emich Charles Ernest
Prince of Leiningen
m Marie, Countess of
Klebelsburg

Feodora
m Ernest, Pri
of Hohenlohe
Langenburg

Prince Ernest Leopold
m Marie Amelie
dr of Grand-Duke
Leopold of Baden

Victoria
m Frederick III
of Germany

EDWARD VII
1841-1910
m Alexandra of Denmark

Alice
m Louis IV
Grand Duke of Hesse

William II
of Germany

Sophie
m Constantine I
of Greece

Victoria
m Louis
of Battenberg

Elizabeth

Irene

Ernest

Alix
m Nichc
of Russi

Albert Victor
Duke of
Clarence

GEORGE V
1865-1936
m Mary of Teck
great grand-daughter
of George III

Louise
Princess
Royal

Victoria

Maud
m Haakon VII
of Norway

EDWARD VIII
Duke of
Windsor

GEORGE VI
1895-1952
m Elizabeth
Bowes-Lyon

Mary
Princess
Royal

Henry

George

Alice
m Andrew
of Greece

Louise
m Gustaf VI
of Sweden

George
Marquess
of Milford
Haven

Louis
Earl
Mountb
of Burn

Margaret

ELIZABETH II

m PHILIP Duke of Edinburgh

Charles
Prince of Wales

Anne

Andrew

Edward

ROYAL FAMILY TREE FF